Get That Job!

MALCOLM HORNBY

Get That Job!

Easy Steps to the Job You Want

3rd Edition

PEARSON
Prentice Hall
BUSINESS

Harlow, England • London • New York • Boston • San Francisco • Toronto • Sydney • Singapore • Hong Kong
Tokyo • Seoul • Taipei • New Delhi • Cape Town • Madrid • Mexico City • Amsterdam • Munich • Paris • Milan

PEARSON EDUCATION LIMITED

Edinburgh Gate
Harlow CM20 2JE
Tel: +44 (0)1279 623623
Fax: +44 (0)1279 431059
Website: www.pearsoned.co.uk

First published as *I Can Do That!* by Delta Management 1993
Second edition 1994
First published as *36 Steps to the Job You Want* by Pearson Education in 1997
Second edition published as *3 Easy Steps to the Job You Want* 2000
This third edition published as *Get That Job!* 2005

ISBN 978-0-273-70212-2

British Library Cataloguing in Publication Data
A catalogue record for this book is available from the British Library

Library of Congress Cataloging-in-Publication Data
Hornby, Malcolm.
   Get that job! : easy steps to the job you want / Malcolm Hornby.—3rd ed.
      p. cm.
   Previous ed. of: 3 easy steps to the job you want. 2nd ed. 2000.
   ISBN 0–273–70212–2
    1. Job hunting—Handbooks, manuals, etc. 2. Career development—Handbooks,
manuals, etc. I. Hornby, Malcolm. 3 easy steps to the job you want. II. Title.

   HF5382.7.H65 2005
   650.14—dc22

                                                             2004060720

10 9 8 7 6 5 4
09

Typeset in 9.5pt Iowan by 70
Printed and bound in Great Britain by Ashford Colour Press, Gosport, Hants.

The Publishers' policy is to use paper manufactured from sustainable forests.

Find a job you love

and you will never have to work a day in your life

Confucius

Publisher's acknowledgements

We are grateful to the following for permission to reproduce copyright material:

General Ability Tests © nferNelson (1988) and *Graduate and Managerial Assessment* © S F Blinkhorn (1985) are reproduced with permission of nferNelson.

Contents

'Would you tell me ... which way I ought to go from here?'
asked Alice
'That depends a good deal on where you want to get to'
said the Cat.

Lewis Carroll *(Alice's Adventures in Wonderland)*

Get that job! – how this book can help

'I can give you a six-word formula for success: 'Think things through – then follow through.'

Edward Rickenbacker

Welcome. This book will help you to take control of your life, plan your career and get the job you want. Since it was first published, it has helped thousands of people to find a new career direction, and to get a new job. Now it's your turn!

I was inspired to write the original version of *Get That Job!* when I first started working with groups of people who had been made redundant in 1990. You know it's often a major 'life-event' such as redundancy, divorce or leaving university, that triggers people into taking stock of what they want to get out of life. But it doesn't have to be. What's needed is the determination that you want the best out of life.

It sounds hackneyed but 'life isn't a rehearsal'. It happens in 'real time'. I'm a firm believer that to get the best out of life you need to take control of your own destiny. *Get That Job! is* a 'self-managed' personal coaching pro-gramme in a book. It will help you to take stock of what you really want out of life. You'll identify what makes you special, you'll set your own career and life goals and you'll learn about techniques which can help you to get the job you want.

How this book can help

I have worked in human resource management for over two decades. In *Get That Job!* 'I've blown the whistle' on many techniques that are used by man-agers, so that you can use the 'inside knowledge' in your jobsearch.

The book contains everything you need – from personality profiling and work–life balance exercises, to practical tips on how to write a CV and letters of application. You'll learn how to access the unadvertised job market, use positive body language, use the Internet, how to make a presentation at an assessment centre . . . and much, much more!

3 easy steps to success

The book is divided into three easy 'steps'.

- **Step 1** contains a number of self-analysis exercises which will help you to develop a greater insight into who you are and what you want out of life.
- **Step 2** will help you to develop your career and life plan and to set your goals.
- **Step 3** contains all the help and advice you'll need to get that job.

Not all the sections or exercises will be relevant to you. Your own career and life situation, age, position, values, etc., will help you decide which areas you need to explore in greatest depth. If you've just been made redundant, are returning to work after a career break, are about to leave school or about to graduate, or are going through a similar major life-change, then you'll probably benefit from working through many of the exercises. On the other hand if you have a clear career and life plan, and a good idea of your next job move, then you'll probably want to concentrate on the tips in Step 3.

Keep an open mind about your future career – you may need to 'reinvent yourself'. I once worked with an accountant who took a 'demotion' from a middle management job to work as a sales representative, so that he could broaden his marketing skills and climb the career ladder in the commercial side of the business. Five years later he was a general manager of one of the company's businesses.

You are responsible for your work-life balance

The responsibility for managing your career and your life is yours. It's not the responsibility of your parents, your teachers, your boss or your organisation . . . or anyone else! Take the initiative.

The exercises in this book will help you develop a greater awareness of what you need to do to create a healthy work–life balance and live the life you want.

It may be tempting to read through the exercises and 'complete them in your head'. Do that as a starting point, but you will gain the most benefit by sitting down pencil in hand!

In my experience, most people spend more time choosing a new car than they ever spend planning what they want to do with the rest of their lives. Use this book to help you to invest some time in yourself. You WILL reap the rewards.

Does it work? Will it be worth it?

YES! It gives me a tremendous buzz when I get phone calls and e-mails from people who have used the techniques in my book to land a job. Like Peter, for instance, a manager who had been unemployed for a year. Peter had applied for hundreds of jobs without success. After using one technique from *Get That Job!* he landed one within a week! Or Heather, a school leaver, who followed the advice in *Get That Job!* and got the first job she applied for, as a trainee veterinary nurse. John had been unhappy in his job in management for over a decade. He was 'liberated' by redundancy and used the techniques from this book to take some easy steps into a job as a college lecturer.

Go for it!! And good luck.

Malcolm Hornby

STEP ONE

Who are you?

Taking stock, taking control

'All things I thought I knew; but now confess the more I know I know, I know the less.'

John Owen

Before we begin

Let me ask you a strange question. Are you more like a frog or a pike? Or aren't you like either of them? Let me explain . . .

Frogs are remarkably adaptable creatures. Apparently, if they are exposed to near-freezing conditions, they can slow down their metabolism and go into hibernation. If you then take one of these frogs and place it in cold water, it becomes more active and increases its metabolism. As the water temperature increases, so does the activity of the frog. The frog makes no attempt to escape from its surroundings . . . even if the temperature of the water is increased to the point where it is boiled to death!

So, while being adaptable, the frog fails to challenge what is happening around it. By being unprepared to move to a different environment, the frog pays the price of its life.

In a similar sort of way, if you take a pike and place it in a large aquarium and then add a few minnows, I am sure you will not be surprised to hear that the minnows are very quickly eaten by the pike. If a glass partition is now placed in the aquarium with the pike in one half and more minnows in the other half, the pike will make attempt after attempt to eat the minnows, but only succeeds in hitting the glass! The pike finally learns that attacking the minnows is an impossible task.

If the glass partition is now removed and the minnows and pike are allowed to swim freely together you might 'naturally' imagine that the pike would resume eating. Surprisingly, it fails to recognise that the environment has changed and does not eat the minnows. In fact the pike will starve to death!

Frog, pike and Lucozade – a recipe for success?

A major first step in your career and life-planning process may be to challenge your 'own life' paradigm:

> **'Paradigm is a set of rules and regulations that describe boundaries and tell you what to do to be successful within those boundaries.'**
>
> *(definition by Joel A. Barker, Discovering the Future, ILI Press)*

But, of course, frogs and pike are very simple animals. Human beings are far more sophisticated and should be more open to change . . . would that it were the case! Just like the frog and the pike, most of us try to find solutions to our problems using our current beliefs about the situation, without recognising the changes that have taken place. For example, many doctors do not recognise 'fringe medicine' such as acupuncture because, in spite of any success, those approaches do not conform to their own training and beliefs.

In business, people are blinded to new approaches by their current beliefs, whether they are developed internally or by competitors. Swiss watch manufacturers dismissed the concept of the quartz watch, in spite of the fact that the first prototype was created in 1967 by the Swiss Watch Federation – their own researchers! This 'blindness' caused the loss of thousands of jobs in the Swiss watchmaking industry.

Similarly, 42 photographic companies rejected Chester Carlson's new photographic process in 1930 because it did not relate to their beliefs surrounding photography. One company did have foresight – the Xerox Corporation.

Most of us can become better at generating new solutions if we:

- listen to others with a totally different view (they probably have a different paradigm)
- listen to our own intuition and have faith in our own absurd ideas rather than suppressing them.

If you cannot generate new solutions, keep your mind open to others' ways of doing things and see if they are worth copying. IBM copied Apple's radical approach to enter the PC market; Wimpy copied McDonald's by becoming counter service rather than table service restaurants.

An excellent example of a successful shift in positioning is the drink Lucozade. In mid-twentieth century Lucozade was known as a glucose drink which helped people to recover after a period of illness – goodness knows how many hospital bedside cabinets had a bottle of Lucozade on them! In the latter part of the century Lucozade repositioned and rebranded itself as an extremely successful 'energy' drink.

What have frogs pike, Lucozade and beliefs got to do with career planning and jobsearching?

Well, everything! Our working environments are changing faster than ever. The rate of change continues to accelerate. A couple of decades ago, no one had heard of HTML, SQL, C++ or Java. Now people who can speak these IT and website assembly languages can almost dictate their salary! There is no 'one way' to plan your career or to find a new job – the keys to maximising your potential are flexibility, keeping an open mind and regarding change as an opportunity, not a threat.

'Seeing is believing' – our beliefs and perceptions about what is right or possible often prevent us from exploring new solutions. You've only got one life. Challenge your life paradigm. Remember what happened to the frog and the pike! Just like Lucozade you may need to reinvent yourself to achieve your goals.

If you tell yourself that you CAN'T achieve your vision of a successful life, then you won't achieve it. *If you tell yourself that you CAN achieve your vision of a successful life, then you might achieve it . . . and you probably will!*

Author's note: the experiments quoted are classic experiments which have been carried out by behavioural scientists.

- The frog – *Shaping Your Organisation's Future: Frogs, Dragons, Bees and Turkey Tails*, J. William Pfeiffer et al., Pfeiffer & Co, San Diego.
- The pike – *Grab Hold of Today,* Eden Ryl, Ramic Productions Film.

I assure you that I have neither boiled frogs, nor starved pike to death – MH.

CHAPTER ONE

The changing world of work

... and your vision of success

'There is nothing permanent, except change'

Heraclitus BC 535–475

That's a quote from a long time ago. So what about now? Well in 1982 no one had a mobile phone because they hadn't been invented! Now it seems as if **everyone** has one – from eight year olds to eighty year olds, and there is an average of almost two mobile phones in use per head of population!

Computer technology and the Internet have given us a new way of doing business. You probably have more computing power on your wrist than existed in the entire world at the start of the 1960s. Computer power is considerably less expensive than it was 30 years ago. If car technology had advanced at the same rate, you could buy a 5 Series BMW for about £1, drive it at the speed of sound and cover the length of the UK on a thimbleful of petrol! And BMW haven't hung around – the current 5 Series model has more computing power in each car than was used to put the first man on the moon!

Technology has changed the way we work for ever. There are now around 25 per cent fewer secretaries employed than ten years ago. Warren Bennis, the management guru, says 'The factory of the future will have only two employees, a person and a dog. The person will be there to feed the dog. The dog will be there to bite the person if they touch any of the controls!' If we think about the changes that have taken place in one area that affects us all – healthcare and the NHS. Many people moan about long waiting lists etc., but if you think about it we have come a long way, particularly in the second half of the twentieth century. And changes continue to take place. How long will it be before we see the Mothercare 'Maternity and Family Planning Unit' in our shopping precincts, or the 'natural' extension of the Virgin empire's involvement in 'retailing' into day-care hospitals providing on-demand minor operations, or Securicor ambulance services? Just my crazy ideas, or are they?

Changes often mean the end of existing jobs and the creation of new work opportunities, as new organisations emerge and existing ones disappear. Is nothing sacred? Well apparently not. If you looked at a list of the USA's top 100 companies in 1900, you'd find only 16 of them exist now. Nearer to home, *The Times* first listed the top 100 UK companies in 1965. Only 30 of the companies from that original list are still there. Size doesn't seem to guarantee success, nor does a good reputation.

It was Leo Tolstoy who first said, 'Our people are our greatest asset'! He was right then, and could not have been more right now! Indeed many organisations now value themselves in terms of their 'human capital'.

Career and life planning is about helping you to capitalise on your own 'human capital assets' and take advantage of present and future job opportunities. In these early chapters we'll spend a lot of time thinking about your strengths and personal qualities, but you must never lose sight of the fact that we live in a world of constant flux and that many 'traditional' jobs are disappearing and new ones emerging.

People like change

Career and life planning is a personal change management process. And of course we've all heard it said in the past that 'people don't like change' haven't we? Well I'm sorry I disagree.

People LIKE change! If people don't like change then why do they look forward to going on holiday, buying new clothes, getting a new car? People like change if it answers the WIFM question in a positive way! **What's in it for me?**

Charles Darwin told us that 'the most successful species are the ones which adapt best to the changing environment. The most successful individuals are the ones with the greatest competitive advantage over the others.' He could have been writing a career and life planning book for the twenty-first century!

But how do you make the most of change? I believe that the most significant element to this is keeping an open mind and having a positive attitude.

Your positive mental attitude

People often have problems in making career plans and developing goals because they impose barriers on themselves. They say to themselves things like 'I could never achieve this', 'that opportunity is not available to me', 'this isn't feasible' etc.

How many times have you heard (or asked!) the question 'Is the glass half full or half empty?' and felt good about the positive 'Half full' answer you've given? Well I'd like you to take your thoughts to a new level. Because, unless you live your life in a vacuum, the glass is ALWAYS full. Sometimes water, sometimes air, sometimes both, sometimes poison, sometimes nectar. 'The glass' is in your hands. The responsibility for making the most of its contents is, to a very large extent, yours. If you adopt the mindset that you CAN make the most of what you've got, then you're halfway to success. In Susan Jeffers inspirational book *Feel the Fear and Do it Anyway*, Susan treats every new life experience as a positive learning opportunity. Even when she contracted breast cancer, she adopted the positive attitude that it gave her a deeper insight into herself. It also gave her the opportunity to meet people whom she had never met before.

Watch the movie *Patch Adams* for a shot of inspiration. It's the true story of a man who turned his life around. Patch was admitted to a psychiatric institution after he had tried to commit suicide. There he realised that he wanted to spend his life helping people. Patch went on to qualify as a doctor and founded the Gesundheit! Institute which is dedicated to bringing fun, friendship and joy to healthcare.

You can develop your positive mental attitude by reading inspirational writings like Kipling's poem *If* or any of the American *Chicken Soup* books. Watch inspirational films like *Top Gun* or *An Officer and a Gentleman* or *Working Girl*, which show peoples' commitment to success.

Many successful sports people develop mental pictures of themselves crossing the winning line first, or scoring that winning goal.

Convince yourself that you are in charge of your own destiny. Believe that you can achieve the success you want, picture yourself achieving it, and you're halfway there!

Failure can teach you to succeed – persevere!

Don't be afraid of failure. Treat it as a learning opportunity. When you're looking for a new job you'll inevitably have to 'kiss a lot of frogs before you find your Prince'. But if you persevere you CAN succeed. Treat each rejection as a step nearer to success. If you don't believe that you can still succeed after failure, then here are some 'failures' that were never going to make it: Coca-Cola, Ford, Gillette and Heinz! They all went on to better things but Coca-Cola sold only 400 bottles in their first year of business, Henry Ford went bust twice before his business successes, and in their first year of trading Gillette sold only 51 safety razors and 168 blades! H. J. Heinz (of beanz fame) went bankrupt, learned the lessons, and did better next time.

Here are some others. Luciano Pavarotti was told that he should follow in his family's footsteps and remain a baker as he would never succeed as a singer. Apparently, John Lennon's Auntie Mimi used to tell him daily that he would never get rich strumming that guitar! Eric Morcambe's mum received a letter from his teacher saying 'I hate to say this, but your Eric will never get anywhere in life'. Hardly any of Schubert's works were performed in his lifetime. The lawyer Abraham Lincoln suffered a series of career failures, but persevered and rose above the rest to become President of the USA.

Charlotte Bronte's first novel was rejected by several publishers before she had *Jane Eyre* accepted and published. All three Bronte sisters had to write under male pseudonyms (Currer, Ellis and Acton Bell) until their novels were 'successful', when their true identity could be revealed.

When I wrote the first edition of this book I was rejected by over 30 publishers. Undeterred I self-published. When I resubmitted the self-published version I got a publishing contract within 24 hours!

Define your own success

When I was in my twenties I once became very disgruntled when a colleague was promoted ahead of me. 'Don't nail your colours to someone else's mast' advised my boss Alan. 'Don't try to live someone else's life.' That advice has stayed with me.

How many of us live lives that are shaped by other people – our parents, our employers, teachers, neighbours, advertisers, priests, friends in the pub . . . the list goes on. There's nothing wrong with taking advice from these people, but when it gets to the point that 'All the children in our family go to medical school' then who's making the choices?

And how do we recognise success? She must be successful – she drives a Porsche. He really must have made it – all of his suits are Hugo Boss. They must be successful – they live in a big detached house and take three holidays a year.

Now I'm not saying that it's wrong to be inspired by people we admire. But we shouldn't try to copy their lives, or live a life that is dictated by the desires of others. My dictionary defines success as 'the favourable outcome of something which one has attempted'. What does success mean to you? What was your kneejerk reaction to that question? A big salary increase? A promotion? A fast car? Seriously, when did you last sit down and write your definition of 'a successful life'? Have you ever done it? You see I believe there are as many definitions as there are people reading this book. And the definition doesn't have to be driven by money. The 15 months I spent working as a volunteer teacher with *Voluntary Services Overseas* in Papua New Guinea count as one of the most successful chapters in my life, in spite of the fact that I was paid only a subsistence-level income.

So what are YOUR criteria for a successful life? What is YOUR life vision? In the space opposite write down the words that come into your head as you develop your definition of success.

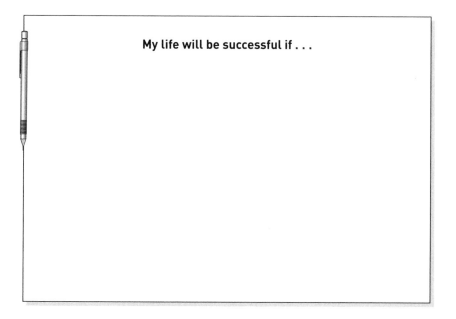

My life will be successful if . . .

'Success is a journey, not a destination.'

Anon.

I have asked this question of hundreds of people at my workshops, and at first was shocked by peoples' answers. I've got used to it over the years. Glazed eyes, dropped jaws and blank expressions. Doh! You'd think I'd asked them to give me the formula for some highly complex chemical, when all I'd really asked was 'What do you want to do with the rest of your life?' I've found most people are too busy with the day-to-day aspects of their lives, to establish a strategic direction and to set life goals.

Another aspect of career and life planning is 'Where do I begin?' Well you've already made a start by thinking about your definition of success. The exercises in this book will help you to think about your past and future life. Keep an open mind as you work through them. As a general rule, people impose more restrictions on themselves than are imposed on them by others.

CHAPTER TWO

Introduce yourself

A five-minute exercise on your past and future

'Know thyself.'

Chilo (BC 560)

Get That Job! is about you. This five-minute exercise will help you to think about your past and future life, both at work and at home.

Few of us are fortunate enough to have our own personal crest or coat of arms, so here is an opportunity for you to design yours! Complete the *Get That Job!* crest on page 13, using the following guidelines. Draw a picture in each of the sections to illustrate:

Section 1 – how you like to spend your leisure time.

Section 2 – something you did recently that you're really proud of.

Section 3 – your greatest professional skill.

Section 4 – your greatest challenge for the next six months.

Banner – write your own personal motto or slogan.

This simple exercise can be very useful to help you to start finding the key to unlock the answer to who you are and who you want to be. Why not take it out of the book, or copy it and put it on the wall where you're planning to work on Getting That Job!

Redundancy and coping with stress

Coping with the pressures of jobsearching

'Worry gives a small thing a big shadow.'

Swedish proverb

Embarking on a jobsearch programme can be challenging, enjoyable and rewarding. For many people the career and life planning, which is part of our jobsearching process, is enlightening. It represents a removal of the blinkers – the first time they have looked at their own life, beyond the end of their nose!

Jobsearching can also be very depressing because: jobsearches for sales-people, accountants, administrators, company directors, recent graduates, career-break returners, teachers, delivery drivers, nurses, computer programmers . . . all look like this:

no no no no no no no no no no
no no no no no no no no no no
no no no no no no no no no no
no no no no no no no no no no
no no no no no no no no no no
no no no no no no no no no no YES

Whatever job you're searching for, jobsearches all look pretty similar! Sometimes there are more noes, sometimes not so many. Since few of us are good at taking NO for an answer, it's hardly surprising that many job-searchers begin their jobsearch with a burst of initial enthusiasm which then turns to anxiety, self-doubt and depression.

Been made redundant?

'Perhaps you have noticed that I have avoided the term (redundant). A man cannot actually be redundant. He can be wrong for a job, his job can disappear from beneath him, his firm may have to contract for financial reasons, but I submit that he cannot actually be redundant. He is a man fresh out of a job, and he is a man who needs to be relocated in a new job. But he remains a man, not an empty space where one once was'.

Malcolm Levene, *The Observer*

First let me apologise to women on Mr Levene's behalf – he seems to have failed to recognise their contribution to the workforce!

If you have been 'made redundant' then I hope the person who handled the process did so in a professional way. I also hope that the following advice will help you.

Whatever euphemisms people may use and whatever the organisational reasons – like 'downsizing', 'financial contraction' or 'mergers' – in reality, the expression we all use as shorthand for what's happened is to say 'S/he's been made redundant'. My father was made redundant after 38 years as a coal miner, my brother-in-law was made redundant after 8 years as a security guard and I was made redundant after 12 years in management.

There can be few people who do not know someone in their close group of friends or relatives who has not been 'made redundant'. Only when it happens to you can you begin to have an inkling of the effect it can have on a person's life.

Those who trivialise redundancy with statements like, 'Well of course if you haven't been made redundant at least once in your career, then you haven't been where the action is', probably haven't been there or they'd be more sensitive.

Now I'm not going to insult you by offering trite and facile advice like 'Remember, tomorrow's another day' and 'Keep smiling and it'll all come good soon'. It might be worth recognising, however, that you're not alone.

You're not the only person who feels like they've received a kick in the ego from a size 12 boot. Common feelings are:

- **Shock** – not being able to appreciate what's happening.
- **Denial** – it's not really happening.
- **Anger** – why me?
- **Lost self-image** – I've failed, my job has gone and I'll never get another.
- **Low self-esteem** – I'm worthless, I'm insecure.
- **Loss** – of direction, colleagues, security and all of the 'comforts' which come from regular work.
- **Rejection** – by the previous employer, by potential employers when they don't acknowledge applications, and by friends when they don't return phone calls.
- **Stigma** – how do my friends and neighbours feel about me now? What will the children tell their school friends?
- **Lack of control** – what if I contact all my friends, identify lots of opportunities, make lots of applications, get interviewed, but still don't get a job?

Now that's cheered you up hasn't it? But you can take control. You now *have* a job. Your job is finding a new job, because it's unlikely that the job is going to come looking for you.

The success of your jobsearch will depend on both the quality and quantity of your efforts. Working through the exercises in this book will help with the quality. You are in charge of the quantity, the number of hours you commit. Don't expect the telephone to start ringing just because you've sent your CV to three or four recruitment agencies.

Persistence does pay off. It is generally believed that when they do get back into work most people get a job with more responsibility, greater job satisfaction and a higher salary than their previous job.

Redundancy policy

If you are contesting the redundancy you might want to ask for a copy of the organisation's redundancy policy. As a guideline a redundancy policy should contain the following.

- A statement of the organisation's intention to provide job security as far as is possible.

- Details of the consultative process for involving employee and trade union representatives.

- The measures which they will take to avoid or minimise redundancies.

- Their selection criteria – this does not have to be based on length of service, LIFO as it is often called (Last In First Out). It may be subject to the retention of key skills, experience and knowledge. They may also include an offer of voluntary redundancy and early retirement options, before selection for compulsory redundancy begins.

- Details of severance terms including statutory payments and ex-gratia payments.

- The appeal procedure for anyone who believes they have been selected or treated inappropriately.

- Any help available to assist the redundant employee to find alternative work – time off to attend interview, training workshops, outplacement programmes.

Notification and consultation

If your organisation is making more than five people redundant, they must consult trade unions and notify them in writing of their intention – even if the number is less than five it is good practice to do so. If they are making more than ten people redundant they must also notify The Department of Trade and Industry.

Fair redundancy

And by this I mean fair in the legal sense of the word. Fair redundancy means that it is a genuine redundancy – employers can't use redundancy as a 'soft option' for getting rid of a poor performer. There must be NO alternative work available. They must follow your organisation's written policy.

Redundancy payment and other rights

Under the *Employment Rights Act of 1996* an employee has a right to receive a redundancy payment, subject to a qualifying period of two years continuous service, if they are dismissed because of redundancy. This normally also includes employees made redundant who have been continuously employed on a series of temporary contracts for two years or more. Remember this is your MINIMUM statutory requirement. Many employers make payments in excess of the minimum requirement and others reduce the qualification time.

Employees with two or more years service are also entitled to receive the appropriate term of notice, time off to look for alternative work and also a trial period, of up to four weeks, in any alternative job (without jeopardising their redundancy rights).

For further information, contact the Redundancy Payments Helpline on 0845 1450004. Or visit DTI's website *www.dti.gov.uk/er/*. ACAS also has some useful tips – the contact details are given below. The following websites represent a goldmine of useful information.

- ACAS – The Advisory, Conciliation Arbitration service – *www.acas.org.uk*
- Bullying – *www.bullying.co.uk*
- Chartered Institute of Personnel and Development – *www.cipd.co.uk*
- Employment law (free access) – *www.emplaw.co.uk*
- Equal Opportunities Commission – *www.eoc.org.uk*
- OneclickHR – many aspects of personnel management – www.oneclickHR.com
- Online employee assistance facility – *www.friendly-ear.com*
- Samaritans – *www.samaritans.org.uk*
- Trades Union Congress – *www.tuc.org.uk*

Jobsearching is stressful

Changing jobs is regarded by 'experts' as being one of the most stressful things in our lives. In day-to-day life we need a certain amount of stress. To some extent, the more stress we have then the better we work (see Figure

3.1). In other words, you need to strike a balance between challenge and having the resources to cope.

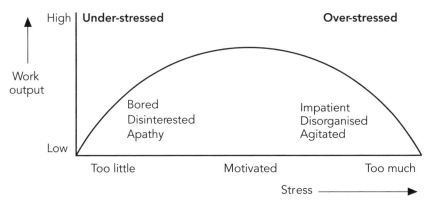

Figure 3.1

To avoid becoming overstressed

- Take a proper break for lunch.
- Have a relaxation break of five minutes every hour or so.
- Take 20 minutes exercise three times a week.
- Manage your time – organise your day so that you can spend some time relaxing with your friends and family.
- Have clear objectives – both long- and short-term – related to what you want to achieve.

Signs of being overstressed

Level 1

- Over-energetic, over-enthusiastic, over-conscientious, overworked, feelings of uncertainty, doubts about coping.
- Too busy to take time off, not knowing when to stop jobsearching, too little time spent with partner/family, frustrated with results.

Level 2

- Irritation, tiredness, anxiety, feelings of stagnation, blaming others.
- Complaints about other people, unable to cope with pressure of handling a number of things at once, working long hours, not managing time efficiently.

Level 3

- General discontent, increasing anger/resentment, lowering of self-esteem, growing guilt, lack of emotional commitment, apathy.
- Not enjoying life, extreme exhaustion, reduced commitment to job-searching, reduced commitment to home.

Level 4

- Withdrawal, illness, feelings of failure, extreme personal distress.
- Avoiding jobsearching activities, avoiding contact with other people, reluctance to communicate, isolation, physical illness, inability to get to sleep/early waking, alcohol or drug abuse.

If you become overstressed

- Try to analyse the problem logically, brainstorm solutions and pick the best option.
- Ask other people for advice.
- Spend time talking to other people – about anything!
- Spend some time on your hobby.
- Take a weekend break.
- Eat proper, regular meals.
- Take some strenuous exercise.
- Reduce your intake of caffeine and alcohol.
- Make love with your partner.
- Indulge yourself in a hot bath, sauna or a massage.

- Socialise with friends.

- Pour out your problems to a good friend.

- Write all your frustrations down on a piece of paper and then tear it up into the tiniest pieces you can.

- Have a good cry or a good shout in the privacy of your home.

- Be creative – write poetry, sing, play a musical instrument.

- Start writing a book!

If it all seems as if it is becoming too much, the Samaritans will lend an ear – the number is in your telephone directory.

Your local GP can also help and many surgeries now have nurses who have received special training in counselling skills. They can be enormously useful in helping you to redirect yourself.

Remember that you're not on your own. Your friends and family love and respect you, not for some job title you once held, but for the person you are.

CHAPTER FOUR

Taking stock

Where have you been? What will the future hold?

'Instead of saying that man is the creature of circumstance, it would be nearer the mark to say that man is the architect of circumstance. It is character which builds an existence out of circumstance. From the same materials one man builds palaces, another hovels; one warehouses, another villas; bricks and mortar are mortar and bricks until the architect can make them something else.'

Thomas Carlyle

In this chapter, which is in two parts, you will think about your life from the time you were born through to the time of your death. Most people find these exercises extremely powerful and enlightening.

If someone close to you has died recently, you may feel uncomfortable thinking about death and may wish to come back to this exercise at a later date. Other people have found, however, that the closeness of their loss has made the exercise even more meaningful.

Part 1

0

•   •

The zero over the left dot represents your birth. Write the year you were born below it.

At what age do you think you will die? This is a difficult question but try to answer it. Above the dot on the right of the line indicate your age at the time of your death. Write the year of your death below the dot.

Now put an arrow on the line to show where you are now – between your birth and your death.

Look at your 'life line'. What are your thoughts about the time that has already passed? What are your thoughts about the time that you have left? What are the three most important things you want to do in the next ten years?

The three most important things I want to do in the next ten years:

Goal A

Goal B

Goal C

Part 2

It sounds morbid, but writing your obituary can help you to think clearly about your past and future life.

Write two obituaries for yourself – one as if you had died yesterday and the other if you were to die ten years from now. You can

- do the exercise alone, or
- prepare your obituaries alone and then share them with your partner or a friend, or
- work with your partner or a friend to prepare obituaries for each of you.

There follows an outline of the details you may want to include. This outline is intended to stimulate your thinking – modify the format if you wish.

Part 2 Alternative: 'Suddenly I'm famous'

If you feel uncomfortable at the thought of the above exercise try this alternative. Imagine that you've suddenly become famous and tomorrow you'll be interviewed by a famous chat show host such as Michael Parkinson or Sir David Frost. Use the sentences from the outline obituaries to help you prepare for the interviewer's questions.

Now do the same for an interview ten years from now!

Obituaries

Complete the following to write your own obituaries.

If I had died yesterday . . .

(Name) _____ died at the age of_____ . He/she was

working on becoming _____ . (Name) _____ had

always dreamed of _____ . He /she had just completed

_____ The thing he/she always wanted to do, but never did, was

_____ .

(Name) _____ will be remembered for_____ .

People will miss most _____

_____

_____

He/she is survived by_____ . The funeral will be_____

(Other information) _____

_____

If I were to die in 10 years' time . . .

(Name) _____ died at the age of _____. He/she was

working on becoming _____ . (Name) _____ had

always dreamed of _____. He /she had just completed

_____The thing he/she always wanted to do, but never did, was

_____ .

(Name) _____ will be remembered for _____ .

People will miss most _____

_____

_____

He/she is survived by_____. The funeral will be _____

(Other information) _____

_____

.

How do they compare? How will you make your 'ten years from now' come true?

CHAPTER FIVE

Managing your finances

Budgeting and where to go for help

'A wise man will make more opportunities than he finds.'

Francis Bacon

Why a chapter on financial management in a book on career and life planning? Well for most people, their salary is their major source of income, yet many people identify their salary requirements in a totally subjective way. Often based on what recruitment ads say, we ignore those offering lower salaries and notice only higher ones. We notice what our contemporaries earn, what the next door neighbour earns, what our brother/sister earns, what our partner earns, etc. with little recognition of what our own needs are!

If personal budgeting skills are one of your great strengths then this chapter may be irrelevant for you. Others will find it very useful!

The exercise will help you to plan your finances and identify your target minimum salary – twice your outgoings total from the six-monthly financial planner, less any annual income.

If you are unemployed and are now the managing director of 'The Me Corporation' then you must do this exercise. After all, you wouldn't want to be employed by a company that didn't do proper financial planning, would you?

Gather together your bank statements, details of mortgage/rent, HP payments, etc., and use the six-monthly financial planner in Table 5.1, to summarise your anticipated income and outgoings for the first month (use pencil).

Table 5.1 Six-monthly financial planner

Budget period _____ **to** _____

[This form should be photocopied and enlarged]

Month												
Budget vs Actual	Budget £	Actual £	Budget £	Actual £	Budget £	Actual £	Budget £	Actual £	Budget £	Actual £	Budget £	Actual £
INCOME: Net Salaries												
Dividends interest												
Other												
INCOME: TOTAL												
OUTGOINGS: Mortgage/rent												
Loans/HP/credit cards												
Household services												
Insurance												
Transport												
Jobsearch												
House/garden												
Food												
Holidays												
Social												
Dependants												
Personal												
Other												
OUTGOINGS: TOTAL												
Bank opening balances												
Bank closing balances												

INCOME
Net Salaries = Salary: self/partner. Redundancy payments. Unemployment benefit. Social security payments.
Other = Tax refunds. Inheritance. Sale of assets. Bonuses.
OUTGOINGS
Mortgage/rent = Regular amount. Endowment insurance.
Loans/HP/credit cards = Total repayments. Items being paid off monthly.
Household services = Water rates. Council tax. Gas. Electricity. Telephone. TV licence/rent. Utilities.
Insurance = House and buildings. Life policies. Medical. House contents. Car(s). Accident/Disability. Pensions.
Transport = Car purchase. Fuel. Service/MOT. Road tax. AA/RAC subs. Repairs/tyres. Bus fares.

Jobsearch = Secretarial services. Equipment. Postage. Paper/journals. Phone calls (free at jobclub if 6 months unemployed).
House/garden = Maintenance. Alterations. DIY. Central heating. Furniture, etc. Garden tools. Plants. Sheds/fences. Domestic appliance maintenance/replacement.
Food = Family. Guests. Pets.
Holidays = Fares. Insurance. Hotels. Car hire. Entertainment. Gifts.
Social = Dining out. Entertainment. Clubs/equipment.
Dependants = Allowances. School fees. Gifts. Maintenance payments.
Personal = Clothes. Hobbies. Gifts. Church charity. Medical. Dental. Optician. Professional sub fees.
Other = Bank charges. Income gains tax contingencies.

27

Now repeat the exercise making your forecasts to build up a picture for the six-month period – this is a realistic period for many jobsearches.

Repeat the exercise at the end of the month and write how much you have spent in the 'actual' column. How are you doing against your budget? Do you need to reforecast?

In carrying out this exercise you'll be able to anticipate those months when the gas bill, TV licence, car tax and car insurance all arrive at the same time! Also, you'll probably realise that with effective budgeting you can still indulge yourself in some of life's luxuries.

If you have got access to a computer and are familiar with using spreadsheets then even better – simply use my headings to develop your own spreadsheet.

Financial tips

These are primarily intended for unemployed jobsearchers but others may find the advice useful.

- Talk to your bank manager (check first to make sure there won't be a charge). They are financial experts and will be able to offer advice on budgeting and on ways to invest a redundancy payment. In this transitionary period of your life, however, be very wary of investments in which you can't get your money back quickly and without penalty. Long-term investments can be looked at when you've settled into the new job.

- Look for the simple ways of saving money – a magazine could cost you £3.00 in the newsagents, but can be read free at the local library. Walking costs nothing and can be a great opportunity to think and plan.

- Talk to an independent financial adviser from a reputable company (beware, 'independent' and 'financial advisers' are often misnomers since they will have a vested interest in earning a sales commission). Talking to an independent financial adviser will help you to review your total financial picture. For example, would it be advisable to take out additional short-term life insurance now that you aren't covered by the company's policy? Is your will up to date? Should I leave my pension in my ex-company's fund or take out a personal pension plan? Tread cautiously.

- Contact your Inland Revenue office – you may qualify for a refund.

- Sign on at the job centre and ask about benefits you are entitled to receive, including any job clubs, adult training and community work opportunities available. If you have been out of work for some time, an up-to-date reference from one of these organisations can be worth its weight in gold.

- Some spare-time activities can also generate a small income. As a child, my daughter Alison was keen on crafts, so she made jewellery and sold it at craft fairs. I like to keep up-to-date with management education, so I have taught a number of the Open University Business School courses. ('Teaching is learning twice!') My friend Roland is keen on keeping-fit, so he trained as a 'step' aerobics instructor and got free membership to his health-club, using his earnings from a weekly class to subsidise his other hobbies.

- Clear out your loft and your garage – a trip to a car-boot sale as a seller can be enormous fun and you'll be amazed at what people will buy! But don't be unrealistic with your prices – remember people are looking for bargains. Or why not try eBay, the Internet auction site?

- Lock away your credit cards! Being unemployed can be extremely expensive. Suddenly you have time on your hands and on your strolls down the high street you'll see lots of bargains you'd never seen before (you were at work!) – you didn't need them then, so do you really need them now?

Lock away your credit cards!

- If you have to sell a 'luxury' asset (for example your classic car, a boat or a piece of jewellery) then plan the sale well in advance so that you can obtain a realistic price. If you have to sell quickly, in desperation, you may accept a much lower price. Not only will you lose out financially but it will depress you as well!

Debts

- Tackle the problem immediately.
- Water, gas, telephone and electricity companies will often accept small instalments, as will credit card companies.
- Contact the Social Security Hotline for free advice (the number will be in the phone book).

When you have predictable and regular income, you can often get away without paying too much heed to the outgoings! When income is substantially reduced, with no immediate prospect of improvement, what you can take control of is the management of your outgoings.

CHAPTER SIX

Your needs and wants in life

Clarifying what you want from life

> 'Ethics, too, are nothing but reverence for life. That is what gives me the fundamental principle of morality, namely, that good consists in maintaining, prompting and enhancing life and that destroying, injuring and limiting life is evil.'
>
> *Albert Schweitzer*

Stage 1

Look at the statements below. Tick the seven that are most important to you.

To feel I have stretched myself/fulfilled my potential ☐
To make worthwhile things or provide a valued service ☐
To be a successful parent ☐
To be respected and acknowledged at work and home ☐
To have a secure and untroubled life ☐
To travel the world/Europe/country ☐
To have as much pleasure as possible ☐
To have no regrets in life ☐
To enjoy love and companionship ☐
To earn as much money as possible ☐
To work overseas ☐
To be free of other people's demands ☐
To be a successful partner to my spouse ☐
To do what I believe to be my duty ☐
To help people less fortunate than I am ☐
To become an acknowledged expert ☐
To have power over other people ☐
To become as famous as possible ☐
Others: _____

Stage 2

Make notes of how you might be able to adapt your life to make sure that you are achieving your needs and wants.

Now rank the seven statements you choose in Stage 1 from most important (1) to least important (7).

1 _____

2 _____

3 _____

4 _____

5 _____

6 _____

7 _____

Keep these in mind when searching for your ideal job.

CHAPTER SEVEN

Your own skills and knowledge

Your unique set of skills and knowledge

'A man's best friends are his ten fingers.'

Robert Collyer

If I asked you to list your skills and the knowledge that might be useful in your new job in the box below, you'd probably say, 'There's far too much room'!

Try it anyway.

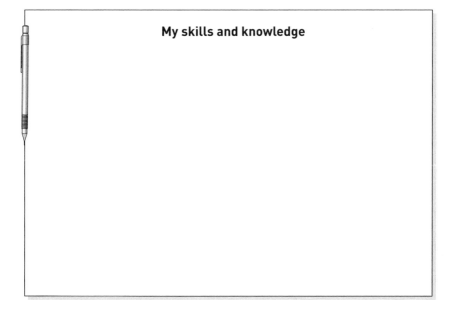

My skills and knowledge

What you have just listed is the tip of the iceberg. You might say 'I've been too busy bringing up a family for the past ten years to develop any new skills' or 'I've been too busy hitting sales targets' or, 'Studying for my degree' . . . to build up additional knowledge.

As we go through life, we develop skills and knowledge, either wittingly or unwittingly. In this chapter you will identify the skills and knowledge you have built up during your life so that you can identify the transferable skills and knowledge to take into your new job.

Look at the three skills banks on the following pages and use a highlighter or tick the skills you believe you have, are good at and enjoy doing. Then complete the 'knowledge reserves' exercise on page 38. These exercises take a considerable time to complete. Do some initial work and then come back to them. Brainstorm with your partner or a close friend. It is worthwhile! Your transferable skills and knowledge bank is the vault holding the currency to obtain your next job.

As you work through these exercises keep thinking of specific examples and how you can expand from the 'general' to the 'specific'. For example if one of your skills is 'writing', then a good example might be that report you did for senior management which swayed a board meeting or that short story you had published.

Time invested on this exercise will reap its rewards when you write your CV, apply for jobs and attend interviews. You will find that you can easily and quickly identify those top skills and knowledge that you have and, importantly, articulate them to a potential employer whether in writing or at an interview.

Learning new skills

'When we stop learning, we stop living.' One of the other things that may come out of this audit is a recognition that there's a gap between where you are now and where you'd like to be – a 'training gap'. Think carefully about how you'd like to close that gap by taking additional training. Go to your library or search the Internet, ask at the careers service, the job centre or your local college to check out the options. Be aware of your own learning style. Some people can study alone and pass exams by reading a few books or taking a correspondence course. Others need the support of others. If you're out of work, you'll probably find that there are many courses that you can attend free of charge. Ask! And don't think you'll be the class dunce just because you haven't studied for 20 years – you'll find that others on the course had the same fear. If you need some inspiration to help you get over your anxiety, read Susan Jeffer's excellent book *Feel the Fear and Do It Anyway*.

Skills bank

Your transferable skills in dealing with people

I am good at and enjoy:

accepting	discovering	informing	pioneering	setting goals	washing
achieving	displaying	initiative	planning	sewing	winning
acting	dissecting	inspecting	playing	shaping	working
addressing	dramatising	inspiring	preparing	showing	writing
administering	drawing	instructing	presenting	singing	
advising	driving	integrating	problem-solving	sketching	
amusing	empathising	interpreting	processing	speaking	
analysing	empowering	interviewing	promoting	studying	
arbitrating	encouraging	investigating	protecting	summarising	
arranging	enforcing	judging	providing	supervising	
assessing	enthusing	keeping-fit	publicising	supplying	
auditing	establishing	leading	purchasing	symbolising	
budgeting	estimating	learning	questioning	synergising	
building	evaluating	lecturing	raising	synthesising	
caring	examining	listening	reasoning	systematising	
chairing	experimenting	maintaining	recommending	taking	
charting	explaining	making	reconciling	taking	
checking	expressing	inventories	recording	instructions	
classifying	financing	managing	recruiting	talking	
coaching	fixing	manipulating	referring	teaching	
communicating	following	mediating	rehabilitating	team-building	
conducting	founding	meeting	relating	telephoning	
consolidating	gathering	memorising	remembering	telling	
consulting	giving	miming	repairing	tending	
controlling	guiding	modelling	reporting	testing	
conversing	handling	monitoring	representing	tolerating	
coordinating	having	motivating	researching	ambiguity	
coping	responsibility	negotiating	resolving	training	
counselling	heading	observing	responding	translating	
creating	healing	offering	restoring	treating	
cultivating	helping	operating	retrieving	trouble-shooting	
debating	identifying	organising	risking	tutoring	
deciding	problems	originating	scheduling	umpiring	
defining	illustrating	overseeing	screening	understanding	
delivering	imagining	painting	selecting	understudying	
detailing	implementing	performing	self-understanding	undertaking	
detecting	improving	persuading	selling	uniting	
developing	improvising	photographing	sensing	updating	
diagnosing	increasing	piloting	serving	upgrading	
directing	influencing			using	

Skills bank

Your transferable skills in dealing with things.

I am good at and enjoy:

achieving	dispensing	illustrating	piloting	retrieving	undertaking
adapting	displaying	implementing	planning	reviewing	unifying
addressing	disproving	improving	playing	salvaging	upgrading
administering	dissecting	improvising	precision	scheduling	using
analysing	distributing	informing	predicting	sculpting	utilising
arranging	drawing	innovating	preparing	selecting	washing
assembling	driving	inspecting	prescribing	selling	weaving
auditing	editing	integrating	printing	sensing	weighing
building	eliminating	interpreting	problem-solving	separating	winning
carving	emptying	inventing	processing	serving	woodworking
checking	enforcing	investigating	programming	setting	working
chiselling	establishing	judging	projecting	setting-up	writing
classifying	estimating	keeping	promoting	sewing	
cleaning	evaluating	lifting	proof-reading	shaping	
collecting	examining	logging	protecting	showing	
compiling	expanding	maintaining	providing	sketching	
completing	expediting	making	publicising	solving	
composing	experimenting	inventories	purchasing	sorting	
conserving	extracting	managing	raising animals	studying	
consolidating	fashioning	manipulating	reading	summarising	
constructing	feeding	manufacturing	realising	supervising	
controlling	filing	massaging	reasoning	supplying	
cooking	financing	memorising	receiving	symbolising	
coordinating	finishing	metalworking	recommending	synergising	
crafting	fixing	minding	reconciling	synthesising	
creating	forecasting	modelling	reconstructing	taking	
cultivating	founding	monitoring	recording	instructions	
cutting	gathering	motivating	recruiting	tending	
deciding	generalising	moulding	reducing	testing and	
delivering	generating	navigating	referring	proving	
designing	getting	observing	rehabilitating	thinking logically	
detecting	giving	obtaining	remembering	tolerating	
determining	growing plants	offering	rendering	ambiguity	
developing	hammering	operating	repairing	training animals	
devising	handling	ordering	reporting	transcribing	
diagnosing	having	organising	representing	translating	
digging	responsibility	originating	researching	treating	
directing	heading	overseeing	resolving	trouble-shooting	
disassembling	identifying	painting	responding	typing	
discovering	problems	photographing	restoring	understanding	

Skills bank

Your transferable skills in dealing with concepts and information.

I am good at and enjoy:

accounting	devising	having responsibility	ordering	representing	thinking logically
adapting	diagnosing	hypothesising	organising	researching	tolerating
administering	digging	identifying	originating	resolving	ambiguity
analysing	discovering	problems	painting	responding	training
animating	displaying	illustrating	perceiving	restoring	transcribing
anticipating	disproving	imagining	piloting	retrieving	translating
ascertaining	dissecting	implementing	planning	reviewing	treating
assembling	distributing	improving	predicting	risking	troubleshooting
assessing	diverting	improvising	preparing	scheduling	typing
auditing	dramatising	increasing	prescribing	searching	updating
budgeting	drawing	influencing	prioritising	selecting	understanding
calculating	editing	initiating	problem-solving	selling	undertaking
charting	eliminating	innovating	processing	sensing	unifying
checking	enforcing	inspecting	programming	separating	uniting
classifying	establishing	installing	projecting	sequencing	upgrading
collecting	estimating	instituting	promoting	setting-up	using
compiling	evaluating	integrating	proof-reading	shaping	utilising
completing	examining	interpreting	protecting	sharing	verbalising
composing	expanding	inventing	providing	sketching	visualising
computing	experimenting	investigating	publicising	solving	weighing
conceptualising	explaining	judging	purchasing	sorting	winning
conserving	expressing	keeping	questioning	storing	working
consolidating	extracting	learning	raising	studying	writing
constructing	filing	logging	reading	summarising	
controlling	forecasting	maintaining	realising	supplying	
copying	formulating	making	reasoning	symbolising	
creating	founding	managing time	receiving	synergising	
deciding	gathering	manipulating	recommending	synthesising	
decision-making	generalising	mediating	reconciling	systematising	
defining	generating	memorising	recording	taking	
delivering	getting	modelling	reducing	instructions	
designing	giving	monitoring	referring	telling	
detecting	guiding	observing	relating	tending	
determining	handling	obtaining	remembering	testing and proving	
developing		operating	reporting		

Now that you have completed these skills banks, asterisk your 'top ten' on each page.

Your knowledge reserves

It would be impossible to list an encyclopaedia of knowledge for you to use as a checklist, but thinking about different times in your life should trigger you to remember knowledge you have acquired.

Complete the chart below with subjects you know something about and enjoy.

Knowledge I have gained from:

School/college/ university	Work	Courses/ apprenticeships/ military
e.g. basic French	e.g. auditing principles	e.g. safety regulations
Reading:	**Computers/video**	**Trial and error/ self-study**
books/ newspapers/ magazines e.g. *Car Values*	e.g. Internet auctions	e.g. marketing principles

CHAPTER EIGHT

Your personality

An enlightening personality profile

'People have one thing in common; they are all different.'

Robert Zend

Psychologists will probably argue for as long as people tread the earth as to whether our personality is 'caught' or 'taught' – whether we inherit it from our parents, or does it develop as a result of our interaction with our environment. Whichever way we get it, we all have one! This exercise will help you to learn more about yours and about your personality 'type'.

Each of the paired blocks on pages 40–1 contains two groups of words. Consider each block in turn and decide which list of words describes you best. There are no right answers and none of the groups of words is 'better' than any other. Do not choose how you would *like* to behave, but how you *know* you behave. You will probably find that some words in each of the paired blocks apply to you. Don't sit on the fence – choose which list is the better description of you. When you have made your choice, circle the appropriate letter – E or I, S or N, T or F, and J or P.

E or I?

E	I
Sociable	Composed
Expressive	Avoid crowds
Think out loud	Like one-to-one meetings
Like socialising in groups	Enjoy your own company
Uninhibited	Keep thoughts to yourself
Enjoy interacting with people	Entertain close friends in intimate groups

S or N?

S	N
Factual	Conceptual
Operate from experience	Look for the 'big picture'
Practical	Innovative
Down to earth	Consider options
Pay attention to details	Enjoy new ideas
Make few errors	Future oriented

T or F?

T	F
Logical	Genuine
Rational	Relationship centred
Objective	Harmonious
Analytical	Base decisions on personal values
Fair	Compassionate
Seek knowledge	Loyal and supportive

J or P?

J	P
Determined	Flexible
Plan	Spontaneous
Organised	Consider all of the options
Purposeful	Adaptable
Set goals	Enjoy variety
Decide quickly	Like to keep options open

Now write the four letters you circled here
(e.g. ENTP, which is my type) __ __ __ __.

This exercise is based on basic personality characteristics and in the following pages you'll find a summary of your profile.

Personality profiles

Clearly there are more than 16 (the number of combinations) 'kinds of people' in the world and I suggest that you now personalise your profile (from those which follow) by crossing out words or expressions which do not describe you and, using a highlighter pen, pick out those that are definitely you.

Your unique profile will help you to communicate to employers the strengths that you can contribute to their organisation.

I've left the section 'Others may be uneasy with' blank on purpose. Try to see yourself the way others may see you and complete this section yourself, in order to build a balanced view of your strengths and limitations. Discuss your profile with your partner or a close friend.

Author's note: No explanation is offered here of the meanings of each of the letters associated with the 'questionnaire'. People trained in administering personality evaluations know what the letters stand for. It is far beyond the scope of this book to train you as a user of personality profiling instruments. Also, because of the simplicity of the exercise, it does not claim to be as accurate as the lengthy personality profiles carried out by psychologists. The type 'descriptors' (for example the architect) are taken from *Please Understand Me* by David Keirsey, an excellent reference (and at *www.keirsey.com* you can take a free 'type' analysis), as is *Life Types* by Sandra Hirsh.

INTP – the architect

Strengths

Creative

Handles change easily

Theoretical

Researches objectively

Idealist

Likes solving complex problems

Imaginative

Innovative

An 'idea' person

Has intellectual insight

As a leader

Prefers to organise things, not people

Writes letters

Enjoys designing change

Enjoys pioneering concepts and ideas

Provides vision and scope

As a team member

Accepts the challenge of complex concepts

Is the 'idea' person

Is able to act as a reviewer of a project

Can incorporate change at any time

Offers creativity and innovation to a project

At work

Needs quiet with occasional privacy

Wants flexibility

Enjoys challenges

Likes an unstructured workspace

Workspace may be cluttered

At home/with friends

Is an earnest and devoted parent

Uses low-key discipline

Likes a quiet home setting

Works at play

Prefers thinking games, e.g. bridge, chess, etc.

Others may be uneasy with

When communicating

Prefers written rather than verbal contact

Wants to discuss the 'big picture'

Likes discussing concepts and ideas

Can be hypothetical and verbose

Enjoys one-to-one contact

Summary

Original

Future-oriented

Inquisitive

Speculative

Reserved

Global thinker

Analytical

Independent

Determined

Uses abstract ideas

ENTP – the inventor

Strengths
Alert to new possibilities
Entrepreneurial
Looks for better ways
Adapts to change
Enjoys learning new skills

Politically astute
Conceptual
Tactical
Likes problem-solving

As a leader
Is sociable and outgoing
Encourages innovation and creativity
in others
Is open to constructive criticism

Relies on others to handle details
Develops models

As a team member
Makes strong initial contributions

Acts as the 'detonator' for the team

Incorporates new ideas

Sees the project reflected through
people
Sees relationships between means
and ends

At work
Works best with independent people
Wants flexible management and guidelines
Needs challenge and reward for risk-taking

Enjoys group activities and gatherings
Likes 'start-ups' or reorganisations

At home/with friends
Is high-spirited and outgoing
Enjoys group chapters and gatherings
Wants a lively environment

Has an 'open-door' policy
Likes flexible relaxation time

Others may be uneasy with

When communicating
Is quick and vocal
Enjoys debate
Is an interesting conversationalist

Is a motivating speaker
Is stimulated by new information

Summary
Understands people
Enjoys new projects
Open-minded
Communicative
Curious and interested

Likes variety and action
Instinctive
Analytical
Enjoys a challenge
Enthusiastic and energetic

INTJ – the scientist

Strengths

Highly practical
Systematic
Individualistic
Mentally quick
Committed

Independent
Resolute
Visionary
Self-motivated
Firm

As a leader

Conceptualises and designs work models
Organises ideas into action plans
Plans strategies for new projects

Is tough-minded and decisive
Instils drive in self and others to attain
goals

As a team member

Pushes for removal of obstacles
Has organisational vision
Is able to systemise goals

Implements new ideas
Streamlines complicated tasks and
procedures

At work

Likes intellectual challenges
Needs privacy for reflection
Wants efficient systems and procedures

Requires a certain amount of autonomy
Prefers a free hand in making decisions

At home/with friends

Combines business with pleasure
Seldom leaves relaxation time to chance
Prefers well-planned activities

Is loyal and caring
Promotes independence in children

Others may be uneasy with

When communicating

Communicates with specific purposes
in mind
Believes that if people 'see it' they
will understand it
Is detached and factual

Collects information visually
Uses logical structure

Summary

Highly practical
Systematic
Individualistic
Mentally quick
Committed
Detached

Independent
Determined
Visionary
Self-motivated
Stable
Logical

ENTJ – The field marshal

Strengths

Enjoys being a leader
Provides structure
Highly analytical
Frank and to the point
Expects hard work

Sets high standards
Likes problem-solving
Admires strength in others
Uses helpful critiques
Prepares for all situations

As a leader

Takes charge
Works for long-term goals
Follows structures and systems

Decisive and tough
Has priorities and deadlines

As a team member

Lays out a blueprint for success
Makes planning logical and workable
Accepts responsibility of explaining to others

Sees that the plan is fully implemented
Breaks projects into elements

At work

Wants to identify personally with the job
Prefers tough-minded colleagues
Prefers an orderly, controlled environment

Seeks both challenge and structure
Wants results to be valued

At home/with friends

Organises and structures family events
Integrates family and career
Enjoys competition

Organises relaxation
Expects dedication and commitment
from partners

Others may be uneasy with

When communicating

Relies on the sixth sense
Looks for the 'structure' of information
Likes to debate an issue

Has a natural clarity of thought and
speech
Is gifted with an insight to language
and its meaning

Summary

Gregarious
Quick-witted
Controlled objectivity
Firm, yet fair

Logical
Verbalises easily and well
Seeks challenge
Strategic

INFP – the questor

Strengths

Creative

Persuasive

Encourages others

Has a sense of timing

Intuitive with people

Is genuinely enthusiastic

Has an awareness of time/history

Is gifted with language

Is a good listener

Is inspired by challenge

As a leader

Prefers to facilitate rather than direct

Seeks out the self-starters

Subtle

Praises other people naturally

Is open to other people's ideas

As a team member

Emphasises need for group or

organisational values

Presents high ideals and a goal of

perfection

Stimulates cooperation

Senses the true needs of others

Is humanitarian

At work

Works well alone

Prefers a company of high integrity

Needs time to reflect

Desires cooperative peers

Wants to be independent

At home/with friends

Relates well to children

Allows others freedom and space

Is easygoing, flows with family needs

Schedules may be subject to change

Is protective of the home and family

Others may be uneasy with

When communicating

Communicates best via the written word

Writes lyrically

Stresses the importance of relationships

Moves people through use of words

Listens with sincere interest

Summary

Idealist

Supporter of causes

Faithful

Searches for the truth

Noble

Honourable

Harmonious

Dedicated to duty

Gentle/polite

Committed

ENFP – the reporter

Strengths

Originates projects

Anticipates needs

Stimulates potential

Concentrates intensely

At ease with others

Appreciates others' input

A perceptive observer

Looks on the bright side

Gives people 'space'

Sees people's potential

As a leader

Knows how to motivate people

Promotes harmony

Conveys the overall value of work to others

Accepts new projects

Uses variety to stimulate others

As a team member

Brings enthusiasm and energy

Is a catalyst who brings people together

Initiates meetings and conferences

Gets things moving from the start

Provides new and interesting aspects and ideas

At work

Enjoys working with colleagues

Prefers an open, friendly atmosphere

Needs variety and challenge

Enjoys an optimistic, idea-oriented workplace

Works best with warm, lively people

At home/with friends

Is charming and gentle with others

Brings surprise and pleasure

Is a devoted and flexible parent

Enjoys bringing people together

Seeks out unusual recreation

Others may be uneasy with

When communicating

Is skilled with the written word

Stresses values

Wins trust through charm and flair

Listens intently

Involves other people in conversation

Summary

Charismatic

Has zest for life

Discerning

Dynamic

Impromptu

Energetic and enthusiastic

Convincing

Intuitive with people

Versatile

Imaginative

INFJ – the author

Strengths

Listens to others

Cooperative

Creative/innovative

Looks to the future

Is determined

Puts integrity first

Consults with others

Patient in relationships

Gentle and accepting

Is loyal

As a leader

Is low key, yet determined

Matches people to the tasks

Wins cooperation from others

Supports causes and ideals

Inspires others to succeed

As a team member

Is an ambassador

Has insight into the needs of others

Works with integrity and consistency

Faces challenge to gain ideals

Helps others to achieve their goals

At work

Needs solitude and room for concentration

Seeks an easygoing environment

Likes room to be creative

Enjoys challenging and novel projects

Wants an organised and harmonious setting

At home/with friends

Is concerned about home comforts

Develops long-term relationships

Enjoys a variety of interests and pursuits

Is a congenial companion

Is subtle in expressing affection

Others may be uneasy with

When communicating

Is an elegant communicator, both written and oral

Prioritises the feelings of others

Considerate of others' views

Has a natural gift for language

Uses relationships as communication values

Summary

Considerate

Highly committed

Calm and sensitive

Harmonious

Warm

Inspires others

Compassionate

Reserved

Accepts challenges

ENFJ – the pedagogue (instructor/educator)

Strengths

Inspirational
Asks for commitment
Stimulates loyalty
Communicates values
Is tactful

Has high standards
Uses an orderly approach
Wins others' respect
Gains cooperation
Is responsive

As a leader

Assigns tasks based on peoples' needs
Promotes group participation
Concerned about feelings of colleagues

Prefers to know who is involved prior
to decisions
Likes to adhere to a plan once it's
underway

As a team member

Provides information about human issues
Relies on personal experiences
and information
Protects the ideas and values of
the organisation

Has an orderly approach
Maintains cooperation within the team

At work

Desires an environment to benefit everyone
Expects surroundings to be settled and
orderly
Likes a value-based, principled
organisation

Enjoys harmony among co-workers
Wants a social, yet professional,
feeling

At home/with friends

Is romantic and devoted
Likes involved and caring relationships
Values harmony in the home

Family and responsibilities come first
Is community/service-oriented

Others may be uneasy with

When communicating

Is openly talkative and social
Generates group involvement
Uses values and traditions as examples

Learns through interrelations
Perceptive

Summary

Loyal
Diplomatic
Harmonious
People-oriented
Expressive

Responsible
Idealist
Supportive
Communicative
Concerned
Expressive

ESFJ – the seller

Strengths

Gentle, yet firm
Fast, thorough worker
Quick to act
Promotes loyalty
Decisive

Unselfish with time
Excellent with people
Tirelessly assists others
Tactful with colleagues
Creates harmony

As a leader

Leads through attention to individuals
Keeps people informed
Adds a 'personal touch'

Sets an example for hard work
Uses experience to support decisions
and actions

As a team member

Promotes team efforts
Resolves conflicts
Is punctual and accurate with data

Respects rules and authority
Is in tune with the needs of
people/employees

At work

Likes goal-oriented colleagues
Prefers friendly, organised surroundings
Likes being where the action is

Needs colleagues who are appreciative
and sensitive
Provides service within specified
structure

At home/with friends

Enjoys socialising and entertaining
Is the centre of an ordered family life
Is a provider for the future

Is warm, caring and committed
Is self-sacrificing and loyal

Others may be uneasy with

When communicating

Is an entertaining conversationalist
Listens with understanding and sympathy
Appreciates others' viewpoints

Is a strong verbal communicator
Obtains information through the senses

Summary

Gregarious
Supportive
Sympathetic
Cooperative
Popular

Respects tradition
Gracious
Personable
Conscientious
Helps friends

ISFJ – the conservator

Strengths

Uses resources wisely
Is knowledgeable
Is just and fair
Is task-oriented
Works tirelessly

Considerate of others
Personalises data
Accepts responsibility
Plans ahead
Simplifies information

As a leader

Is consistent and orderly
Sets priorities around people
Is focused and detailed

Uses personal influence discreetly
Preserves traditional rules and
procedures

As a team member

Is thorough and painstaking
Carries out detailed and routine tasks
Makes effective decisions and takes action

Personalises the goals and projects
Provides stability and followthrough

At work

Prefers a secure working environment
Needs time to be alone
Wants order and routine

Appreciates accurate and conscientious
colleagues
Enjoys direct physical involvement with
work

At home/with friends

Is devoted to the family
Enjoys traditional family activities
Maintains impeccable surroundings

Relaxes when work is finished
Values personal belongings

Others may be uneasy with

When communicating

Uses examples and samples to
communicate
Is direct and to the point
Is friendly and patient

Looks for clear-cut contrasts
Writes things down

Summary

Sympathetic
Detailed and factual
Conscientious
Respects tradition
Sense of history
Impromptu

Down to earth
Sense of justice
Service-oriented
Meticulous with detail
Practical and organised

ESFP – the entertainer

Strengths

A keen observer

A 'do it' person

Is optimistic

Is enthusiastic

Advocates harmony

Accepts people for who they are

Generous with time

Is sociable

Understands most people

As a leader

Handles crises well

Facilitates the interaction of people

Promotes goodwill and teamwork

Is attentive to the expectations of others

Encourages agreement and compromise

As a team member

Brings in enthusiasm and cooperation

Offers action and excitement

Does it now – doesn't linger

Takes account of the needs of people

Supports the organisation loyally

At work

Likes an energetic, yet easygoing atmosphere

Prefers to focus on present realities

Prefers adaptable and lively colleagues

Likes the centre of action to be around people

Wants attractive surroundings

At home/with friends

Is generous to others

Enjoys a beautifully decorated home

Is sentimental and enjoys pleasing others

Is sociable and spontaneous

Likes a varied and busy day

Others may be uneasy with

When communicating

Is a straightforward communicator

Uses a simple and sensitive approach

Enjoys talking

Stimulates conversation

Relates today's situations to people

Summary

Open and outgoing

Pleasant

Cooperative

Positive and upbeat

Empathises

People-oriented

Tolerant

Realistic

Quick to act

Adaptable

ISFP – the artist

Strengths
Receptive to others
Is generous with time
Is open-minded
Generates trust in others
Respects others' feelings

Is unconditionally kind
Is the eternal optimist
Solves problems
Is understanding and trusting

As a leader
Praises and encourages
Monitors group performance
Is adaptable and cooperative

On hand in a crisis
Is able to utilise the strengths of
others

As a team member
Is cooperative
Brings focus to people's needs
Understands the need for teamwork

Builds systems around productive
people
Provides service to a project

At work
Needs a private, unconfined space
Wants compatible colleagues
Desires flexibility to be productive

Likes an aesthetic work environment
Is concerned about people's actions

At home/with friends
Enjoys private leisure time
Is personable and humorous
Makes time for simple pleasures

Needs to maintain relationships
Enjoys solitary pursuits

Others may be uneasy with

When communicating
Is in tune with the needs of others
Prefers calm, controlled conversations
Looks for meaning in people's actions
and words

Listens before speaking
Likes quiet, considerate colleagues

Summary
Gentle and considerate
Quiet disposition
Has an inner intensity
Can act spontaneously
Is in touch with reality

Unpretentious
Sensitive to others
Artistic
Unassuming
Cooperative and balanced

ESTJ – the administrator

Strengths

Plans ahead
Declares views openly
Uses experience
Is a good organiser
Follows through

Meets deadlines
Is a prompt decision-maker
Respects authority
Is tough-minded
Manages and controls

As a leader

Is direct and to the point
Applies past experiences to resolve
problems
Uses rewards with employees

Takes charge
Firm yet open to ideas

As a team member

Works well with policies and procedures
Is effective at controlling time spent on
a project
Understands the importance of full
cooperation

Is prepared to act when called upon
Uses a systematic approach to a
challenge

At work

Enjoys being in charge
Likes to work alongside dedicated
colleagues
Prefers defined projects

Prefers stable and predictable
surroundings
Likes to work with, and through,
people

At home/with friends

Is community-minded
Is prudent and conservative
Treats home as his/her castle

Mixes business with pleasure
Has strong family ties

Others may be uneasy with

When communicating

Is an effective verbal communicator
Is a good sounding board for others
Is crisp and direct

Communicates with facts
Wants outlines rather than details

Summary

Deals in reality
Goal-oriented
Responsible
Stable
Systematic

Conscientious
Organiser
Thorough
Decisive
Logical and objective

ISTJ – the trustee

Strengths

Knows the rules
Follows guidelines
Likes structure
Is dependable
Accepts responsibility

Adapts to new routines
Takes charge
Team-oriented
Puts work before play
Meets deadlines

As a leader

Sets the standard for others
Is goal-oriented and expects others to be
Controls resources and costs

Is direct and succinct
Supports existing systems, structures
and standards

As a team member

Organises and plans
Follows schedules
Meets deadlines

Respects traditions and rules
Takes responsibility for projects

At work

Plans the work and works to the plan
Wants details
Likes a task-oriented, quiet environment

Prefers involvement
Expects work to be orderly

At home/with friends

Is trustworthy and dedicated
Committed to the family
Expects rules to be adhered to

Is a pillar of strength
Is conservative

Others may be uneasy with

When communicating

Likes visuals – flowcharts, diagrams
and graphs, etc.
Direct and to the point
Is logical and sequential

Respects agendas
Relates to experience

Summary

Thorough
Factual
Tangible
Consistent
Committed

Reliable
Reserved
Orderly
Systematic
Down to earth

ISTP – the promoter

Strengths
Is straightforward
Handles risks
Is a negotiator
Initiates
Responds quickly

Is results-oriented
Remembers data and facts
Takes action
Mediates problems
Is a realist

As a leader
Is direct
Is attentive at meetings
Handles problems quickly

Takes charge in emergencies
Uses persuasion to speed things along

As a team member
Acts as a go-between in negotiations
Adapts to working with all types
Supports projects with data and facts

Is able to adapt to last-minute changes
Likes being the troubleshooter

At work
Wants minimal bureaucracy
Includes time for fun while working
Wants an attractive work environment

Likes to master technical problems
Desires results-oriented colleagues

At home/with friends
Is active with friends and family
Enjoys both personal and group activities
Has wide outside interests

Is a fun-loving charmer
Likes impromptu projects and parties

Others may be uneasy with

When communicating
Uses both oral and visual communication
Is personable and engaging
Enjoys discussing plans and operations

Likes a 'real' debate
Is perceptive of body language

Summary
Easygoing
Prepared for action
Lively and quick
A realist
Resourceful

Spontaneous
Versatile
Entertaining
Persuasive
Alert

ESTP – the artisan

Strengths

Is receptive to others
Keeps calm in a crisis
Is trusting
Is a fount of knowledge
Is dextrous

Has technical insight
Is a risk-taker
Is a troubleshooter
Gets things done
Is action-oriented

As a leader

Wants subordinates to follow
their example
Manages work and people with
minimal controls
Is able to respond to emergencies

Likes people to build action groups
Seeks new ideas and methods

As a team member

Enjoys compiling relevant technical data
Has a sense of priority to achieve a goal

Is able to adapt to last-minute changes
Will work within specific guidelines
Wants to be involved in new projects

At work

Likes project-oriented operations
Likes to work with action-oriented people
Wants to be involved

Likes dealing with things rather than
people
Prefers flexible rules and procedures

At home/with friends

Is private and protective of the family
Is responsive and realistic
Is attentive to the needs of others

Is relaxed and easygoing
Enjoys repairing things for the family

Others may be uneasy with

When communicating

Likes talking to people one-to-one
Is direct and yet open with others
Seeks essential facts

Likes technical data
Learns by doing

Summary

Reserved
Factual
Logical
Adaptable
Independent

Practical
Down to earth
Analytical
Prudent
Spontaneous

CHAPTER NINE

Your communication and working style

A personal insight

'Make the most of yourself, for that is all there is for you.'

Ralph Waldo Emerson

Effective communication with others is a key skill for helping you to achieve your career and life goals. In this exercise I'd like to introduce you to a process which will give you a deeper understanding of your communication and working style and help you to understand how to get along better with other people.

You don't need me to tell you that people come in all shapes, sizes and personalities! For example, some people are the life and soul of the party, dress flamboyantly and speak in loud, fast voices – get two of them together and it's almost a competition to see who can burst the other's eardrums! Try approaching one of these people in a timid, mild-mannered and factual way and you're unlikely to make an impression.

Other people like to conduct business in a very formal way, they're abrupt and to the point and only interested in 'the bottom line.' Approach a meeting with these people with a barrage of 'friendly' questions about family, hobbies and what they did during the weekend and you've probably burned up 80% of the time they've allocated for the meeting!

It is often said that if you want to understand people and get along with them better, then the best starting point is to understand yourself.

Communication Style Inventory – SADI © on the following pages, will help you to understand your own preferred communication style.

Be honest and realistic when completing your answers. Do not complete the inventory as you think you *should* act, or as you would *like* to act, but how you believe you really DO act in work situations. Give each question considered thought. There is no time limit and there are no trick questions. Once you have completed the inventory you will be able to analyse your results and read about your preferred communication style.

Communication Style Inventory – SADI ©

CSI – SADI contains 28 pairs of statements, which relate to the way people behave in work situations. For each pair of statements, you have five points to distribute between the two alternatives (A and B). Base your answers on your knowledge of your behaviour. Your scores must be whole numbers – no fractions!

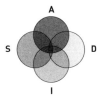

How to score your answers. If . . .

A is very characteristic of me and B is very uncharacteristic	A = 5 and B = 0
A is fairly characteristic of me and B is fairly uncharacteristic	A = 4 and B = 1
A is more characteristic of me than B	A = 3 and B = 2
B is more characteristic of me than A	B = 3 and A = 2
B is fairly characteristic of me and A is fairly uncharacteristic	B = 4 and A = 1
B is very characteristic of me and A is very uncharacteristic	B = 5 and A = 0

Remember, the numbers you assign to each pair of statements must add up to 5

Example

When I think about my own decision-making style: A is fairly characteristic of me. B is fairly uncharacteristic. So I would mark my responses as follows:

17A _4_ am fast-paced in my decision-making

17B _1_ take time to reach well thought-out decisions

When thinking about my behaviour with other people at work, I:

1A _____ prefer an informal and relaxed work environment

1B _____ prefer a formal and businesslike work environment

2A _____ am slow and deliberate in my actions

2B _____ am fast and spontaneous in my actions

3A _____ am adaptable in my approach to people and situations

3B _____ am predictable in my approach to people and situations

4A _____ am disciplined and structured about the way other people use my time

4B _____ am flexible about the way other people use my time

5A1 _____ express my opinions freely in groups, without being asked

5B _____ tend to contribute in groups, when invited to do so

When thinking about my behaviour with other people at work, I:

6A _____ am usually willing to negotiate the outcome of situations

6B _____ am usually reluctant to negotiate the outcome of situations

7A _____ focus on the feelings and opinions of others during discussions

7B _____ focus on the facts and business issues during discussions

8A _____ respond to conflict situations slowly and indirectly

8B _____ respond to conflict situations quickly and directly

9A _____ am usually willing to change my opinions and ideas

9B _____ am not usually willing to change my opinions and ideas

10A _____ keep my personal feelings and thoughts private

10B _____ discuss my feelings freely with others

11A _____ take the initiative to introduce myself in social situations

11B _____ tend to wait for others to introduce themselves to me in social situations

12A _____ am flexible in my approach to dealing with people and situations

12B _____ am predictable in my approach to dealing with people and situations

13A _____ prefer to work in a group with others

13B _____ prefer to work on my own

14A _____ am cautious and predictable in my approach to risk and change

14B _____ am dynamic and unpredictable in my approach to risk and change

15A _____ quickly adapt to new systems and working practices

15B _____ like to take my time to adapt to new systems and working practices

16A _____ prefer to focus primarily on business ideas and results

16B _____ prefer to focus primarily on people and their feelings

17A _____ am fast-paced in my decision-making

17B _____ take time to reach well-thought-out decisions

18A _____ like to cope with many different situations at the same time

18B _____ prefer to handle one thing at a time

When thinking about my behaviour with other people at work, I:

19A _____ tend to get to know many people personally

19B _____ tend to get to know only a few people personally

20A _____ tend to keep my opinions to myself, and prefer to offer them when asked

20B _____ state my opinions freely without being asked

21A _____ tend to make my decisions based on facts or evidence

21B _____ tend to make my decisions based on feelings or opinions

22A _____ like to actively seek out new experiences and situations

22B _____ tend to choose known or familiar situations and relationships

23A _____ am an intuitive decision maker

23B _____ am a rational decision maker

24A _____ am non-confrontational and comfortable with a slow pace

24B _____ am direct with others and can be impatient when things move slowly

25A _____ share my personal feelings and emotions in conversation

25B _____ control my personal feelings and emotions in conversation

26A _____ tend to dominate conversation in group discussions

26B _____ tend to make infrequent well-thought-out inputs in group discussions

27A _____ am more interested in people's opinions than facts

27B _____ am more interested in facts than people's opinions

28A _____ tend to move at a controlled pace

28B _____ tend to move at a fast pace

C S I – SADI and the four circle model are copyright Delta-Management.co.uk Ltd.

When you have completed the inventory and **checked to make sure that the score for each pair of questions adds up to five,** transfer your scores to the table on page 64. **Please take care when transferring your scores as the A–B order changes in some of the rows.**

E	R	S	L	SAH + (These are positive numbers)	SAL – (These are negative numbers)
1A	1B	2B	2A	3A +	3B –
4B	4A	5A	5B	6A +	6B –
7A	7B	8B	8A	9A +	9B –
10B	10A	11A	11B	12A +	12B –
13A	13B	14B	14A	15A +	15B –
16B	16A	17A	17B	18A +	18B –
19A	19B	20B	20A		
21B	21A	22A	22B		
23A	23B	24B	24A		
25A	25B	26A	26B		
27A	27B	28B	28A		
E Total	R Total	S Total	L Total	SAH Total +	SAL Total –

Compare your **E** and **R** scores. Which is higher? Write the higher score in the space below and circle the corresponding letter:

_____   **E**   **R**

Compare your **S** and **L** scores. Which is higher? Write the higher score in the space below and circle the corresponding letter:

_____   **S**   **L**

To calculate your style adaptability score combine your SAH and SAL scores to give you a number ranging from +30 to –30. SAH are positive numbers, SAL are negative numbers.

STYLE ADAPTABILITY SCORE: _____

Your communication style

By completing the **Communication Style Inventory–SADI** © you have given an indication of your preferred way of communicating with others.

By the time we reach mid-to-late twenties, most people have become comfortable with a particular style. Understanding your own style and the styles of others can help to make meetings with other people more productive. The main objective of understanding communication style is to help you to develop style adaptability in dealing with others.

Calculating your **C S I–SADI scores will show your preferred communication style. This should help you to understand how you might 'come across' to others, and will help you to plan how you can deal more effectively with other people. If your higher scores are:**

E and L your style is	**S**upporter
L and R your style is	**A**nalyst
R and S your style is	**D**irector
E and S your style is	**I**nstigator

There is no best style! And as you read about the four styles, you'll probably say 'I can be all of these!' And you probably can! The fact is that we all have our own preferred style. All of us have the potential ability to adopt different styles at various times. What you have identified by completing the inventory is your 'comfort zone'.

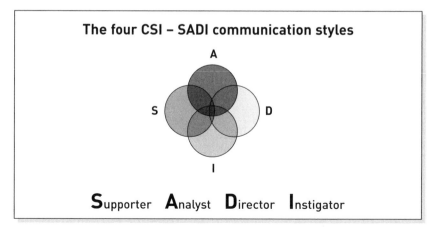

The four CSI – SADI communication styles

Supporter **A**nalyst **D**irector **I**nstigator

As you can see from the four circle SADI diagram on page 65 there are four communication style comfort zones and they all overlap in the middle. At different times we can adopt any of the communication styles, but most of the time we prefer to stick to *our* comfort zone. You'll probably find that if you move out of your comfort zone, then it is easier to move to the circles either side of your comfort zone. It's usually most difficult to move to the circle that's directly opposite yours. That is because the communication style which is the direct opposite of yours, is furthest from your comfort zone.

Understanding your **C S I–SADI** ommunication style can help you relate to other people in a better way. By knowing your own style, and knowing how to recognise the style of others, you can improve communication.

Of course there are two sides to every coin. For example the self-confident Director may be interpreted as an insensitive steamroller by other people, and the accurate Analyst may be seen as pedantic and nitpicky. The helpful Supporter can be considered as weak and wishy-washy whilst the inspiring Instigator may be seen as insincere and shallow. As you read more about your preferred style on the following pages, try to think about how other people might interpret your behaviour.

Your communication style can also give you some clues as to your preferred working environment. It can also give some ideas on the kind of work you may prefer. Descriptions of the four styles are given on the following pages.

Supporter

Supporters are 'naturals' when it comes to relating to others. You are: cooperative, a natural team player, slow-paced, trusting, quiet, supportive, friendly, a good listener, non-confrontational, sensitive, patient, understanding, generous, helpful, personable and unassuming. People see your communication style as: quiet, supportive and helpful, accommodating, loyal and able to empathise.

You probably prefer a working environment where: you are allowed or encouraged to think ideas over before implementing them. You are able to stand back from events and listen and watch before making decisions; you are allowed to think before acting or commenting; you can carry out research and investigate, assemble information and probe to get to the bottom of things; you are asked to produce carefully considered analyses and reports; you can reach a decision in your own time without pressure and tight deadlines; you have the opportunity for regular contact with a variety of people.

You probably won't enjoy working where: you are forced to stand in the limelight like having to act as leader / chairman / presenter; you are involved in situations, which require action without planning; you are pitched into doing something without warning, like producing an instant reaction or an instant idea; you are given insufficient data on which to base a conclusion; you are given instructions of how things should be done, without involving others; you are worried by time pressures, or rushed from one task to another; you have to take short cuts or do a superficial job.

Questions to ask yourself: will I be given adequate time to consider, assimilate and prepare my work? Will there be opportunities and facilities to organise my work? Will there be opportunities to work with a wide variety of other people and incorporate their ideas into my work? Will I be under pressure to work to tight deadlines, which may result in sloppy work?

Some job ideas: admin assistant, bartender, coach, counsellor, diplomat, general practitioner, mediator, minister, missionary, nurse, psychologist, public relations, receptionist, salesperson, social worker, teacher.

The strengths you'll bring to the job: you facilitate team working and cooperation; you diffuse conflict; you create a friendly impression with people; you create a relaxed and unruffled atmosphere; you are loyal.

Analyst

Analysts like to consider all of the options and move slowly, but precisely. You are: logical, a natural planner, quality focused, analytical, organised, exact, a perfectionist, structured, a good listener, independent, controlled, cool, non-aggressive, disciplined, deliberate and businesslike. People see your communication style as: structured and organised, quiet and unassuming, factual and logical, practical and controlled, cautious and conscientious.

You probably prefer a working environment where: you work within a system; you can methodically explore the associations and interrelationships between ideas, events and situations; you have the chance to question and probe the basic methodology, assumptions or logic, like checking a report for inconsistencies; you work with high calibre people who ask searching questions, which stretch you intellectually; you are in structured situations with a clear purpose; you are required to understand and participate in complex situations.

You probably won't enjoy working where: you have to do things without a context or apparent purpose, like doing things, just for the fun of it; you have to work in situations, that focus on emotions and feelings; you are involved in unstructured work where there is a lot of ambiguity and uncertainty; you have to make decisions without guidelines or policies; you find the work shallow or gimmicky and without real purpose; you have to work with people of a lower intellectual calibre.

Questions to ask yourself: will there be lots of opportunities to question my work? Is the work clear, structured and purposeful? Will I work on complex ideas and concepts that are likely to stretch me? Are the working systems tested, sound and valid?

Some job ideas: accountant, building inspector, business analyst, city planner, computer programmer, data processor, efficiency expert, engineer, investigator, IT/technical salesperson, Justice of the Peace, military strategist, museum curator, proof-reader, quality control inspector, researcher, secretary, administrator, solicitor, surgeon, statistician.

The strengths you'll bring to the job: your attention to detail and production of top-quality work; logical and analytical work methods; the ability to do tedious work, for long periods alone.

Director

Directors prefer to be in control of situations. You are: businesslike, a natural leader, goal-centred, fast-paced, task-oriented, assertive, decisive, confident, determined, competitive, independent, straightforward, direct, an achiever, challenging, correct, you take the initiative, confront, are quick, opportunistic and forceful. People see your communication style as: in-charge, efficient, direct, quick and controlled.

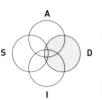

You probably prefer a working environment where: you are given autonomy in decision-making; you are in charge; you have the chance to try out and practise things, and get feedback from someone you respect because of their expertise; you respect your boss as an expert; you can implement your ideas quickly; you work on practical issues, such as drawing up action plans, suggesting short cuts and giving tips; you learn techniques for doing things with obvious practical advantages, such as how to do a job more quickly, how to make a good first impression, or how to deal with awkward people

You probably won't enjoy working where: you find the work irrelevant, esoteric or unrelated to an immediate need; you cannot see the results of your efforts; you cannot see immediate relevance or practical benefits; you feel colleagues are out of touch with reality, who are pompous, or live in ivory towers; there is no practice or clear guidelines on how to do it; people go round in circles without getting anywhere; there are lots of politics and protocols; you can't see a relationship between your work and the real world.

Questions to ask yourself: Will I be given a free rein to do things my way? Will there be lots of practical help and resources? Does the job address real issues? Will I have a boss who knows how to / can do it? Will I be stretched?

Some job ideas: business coach, business manager, conductor, director, foreman, head waiter, military officer, negotiator, own business, personnel manager, pilot, police officer, president, project leader, sales manager, security guard, shop steward, supervisor.

The strengths you'll bring to the job: you can take charge and set goals; you can finish a lot of jobs quickly and work to tight deadlines; you take control and don't shy away from conflict.

Instigator

Instigators like to get things going and then move on. You are: inspiring, a natural risk-taker, ideas-driven, creative, innovative, flexible, visionary, spontaneous, enthusiastic, free-spirited, energising, emotional, friendly, sociable, intuitive, an initiator, political, excitable and a doer. People see your communication style as: Comforting and fun, people-centred, ambitious and competitive; inspiring and exciting; motivating.

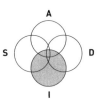

You probably prefer a working environment where: there are new experiences, problems and opportunities; you can immerse yourself in short projects with tight deadlines; the environment is exciting and things change regularly with a range of diverse activities to tackle; you have a lot of the limelight / high visibility, such as chairing meetings, leading discussions and giving presentations; you are allowed to generate ideas without constraints of policy or structure; you are thrown in at the deep end with a difficult problem; you are involved with other people brainstorming ideas and solving problems, as part of a team; you feel you are free to 'have a go', to try new ideas and ways of doing things.

You probably won't enjoy working where: you have a passive role, with no involvement in decision-making; you are required to assimilate, analyse and interpret lots of data; you have to work alone most of the time; you have to work on theoretical concepts; you have to repeat the same activity over and over again; you have precise instructions, policies and procedures to follow with little room for your interpretation; you are required to do a pedantic job and attend to lots of detail.

Questions to ask yourself: Will I learn something new in the job that I didn't know or couldn't do before? Will there be a wide variety of different activities? Will it be OK to have a go, let my hair down, make mistakes and have some fun? Will I work on tough problems and challenges? Will I get a chance to demonstrate my success?

Some job ideas: activities leader, advertising account executive, architect, artist, builder, business strategist, chief executive, estate agent, events director, explorer, headhunter, landscaper, performer, presenter, project director, property developer, public relations, tour guide, writer.

The strengths you'll bring to the job: your creative ideas and talents; versatility and an ability to win people over; innovative and unconventional thinking. Free-spirited risk-taking; an ability to act quickly.

The four CSI–SADI communication styles

Supporters	Analysts
<ul><li>Need cooperation, personal security and acceptance</li><li>Uncomfortable with and will avoid conflict</li><li>Value personal relationships, helping others and being liked</li><li>May sacrifice their own desires to win approval from others</li><li>Prefer to work with other people in a team effort, rather than individually</li><li>Have an unhurried reaction time and prefer the status quo</li><li>Are friendly, supportive, respectful, willing, dependable and agreeable</li><li>Are people-oriented</li><li>Use opinions and stories rather than facts and data</li><li>Speak slowly and softly</li><li>Lean back while talking and do not make direct eye contact</li><li>Have an informal posture and an animated expression</li><li>Perceived as conforming, unsure, pliable, dependent and awkward</li><li>Have homely offices – family photographs, plants, etc.</li></ul>	<ul><li>Concerned with being organised, having all the facts and being careful before taking action</li><li>Need to be accurate and to be right</li><li>Are precise, orderly and methodical and conform to standard operating procedures, organisational rules and historical ways of doing things</li><li>Have a slow reaction time and work slowly and carefully</li><li>Are perceived as serious, industrious, persistent and exacting</li><li>Are task-oriented</li><li>Use facts and data</li><li>Tend to speak slowly and want lots of information</li><li>Lean back while talking and use their hands infrequently and do not make direct eye contact</li><li>Control their facial expressions</li><li>May be seen as stuffy, indecisive, critical, picky and moralistic</li><li>Are comfortable in positions in which they can check facts and figures and be sure they are right</li><li>Have neat / well-organised offices</li></ul>
Instigators	**Directors**
<ul><li>Enjoy involvement, excitement and action</li><li>Are social, stimulating and enthusiastic and are good at involving and motivating others</li><li>Have ideas and are future orientated</li><li>Have little concern for routine</li><li>Have a quick reaction time</li><li>Need to be accepted by others</li><li>Tend to be spontaneous, outgoing and energetic</li><li>Focus on people rather than tasks</li><li>Use opinions and stories rather than facts and data</li><li>speak and act quickly; vary vocal inflection</li><li>Lean forward, point and make direct eye contact</li><li>Use their hands when talking</li><li>Have a relaxed bodily posture and an animated expression</li><li>Show their feelings in their faces</li><li>Are perceived by others as excitable, impulsive, undisciplined, dramatic, manipulative, ambitious, overly reactive and egotistical</li><li>Have disorganised offices that may have leisure equipment such as golf clubs or tennis racquets</li></ul>	<ul><li>Are action- and goal-oriented</li><li>Need to see results</li><li>Have a quick reaction time and are decisive, independent, disciplined, practical and efficient</li><li>Use facts and data</li><li>Speak and act quickly</li><li>Lean forward and point and make direct eye contact</li><li>Have a rigid body posture</li><li>Have controlled facial expressions</li><li>Do not want to waste time on personal talk or preliminaries</li><li>Perceived as dominating or harsh and severe in pursuit of a goal</li><li>Are comfortable in positions of power and control</li><li>Have businesslike offices with certificates and commendations on the wall</li></ul>

Style adaptability

There is no 'best' style. The key to using this process is *style adaptability*. Around a quarter of the population have a similar 'style' to yours and so you will probably find that you are comfortable with them.

You have probably noticed that some people are naturally very adaptable and are able to accommodate easily to the needs of other people. Others are less skilled and are often seen as inflexible, or maybe even downright difficult! *By developing your adaptability skills, you will be able get on with more people.*

Why is this so important? As a private individual you have complete freedom of choice in whom you socialise with, who you like and who you don't like. But to be successful at work you *must* have the skills to get along with all kinds of different people. If you know what makes *you* tick, and also have an insight into what makes your subordinates, colleagues and managers tick, then you've made a pretty good start on the journey!

The people you probably find it most difficult to relate to naturally are your 'opposites'. Study the characteristics of your opposite style.

Think about how *you* can adapt your behaviour (i.e. improve your style adaptability) next time you meet someone with your 'opposite style'. For example, Analysts may need to warm up when dealing with Instigators and be prepared to be interviewed over a pie and a pint – just because the surroundings are informal does not make the meeting any less important. Instigators need to be specific and factual in their contacts with Analysts – they should be precise about what they say and give them time to assimilate it, and make decisions. Supporters need to get to the point when dealing with Directors – all that chit-chat about family and hobbies can be lost on Directors. Directors need to slow things down and indulge in friendly conversation when meeting Supporters in order to develop a trusting relationship.

Style adaptability is a skill

Now transfer your style adaptability score from the inventory on page 64 onto the scale here.

+30	+25	+20	+15	+10	+5	−5	−10	−15	−20	−20	−25	−30

High   0   Low

Style adaptability is a skill, which can be learned and developed. Some people are 'naturally' more adaptable than others. By being more adaptable you'll make other people feel more comfortable about being in your company. Your score is not fixed – you can develop your style adaptability and the more you adapt, the easier it becomes to get on with different people. How did you score?

Low score (0 to −30)

This may mean that you are reluctant to 'bend' to the needs of others – your approach is 'take me as I am', or 'what you see is what you get'. You like to do things for *your* reasons, rather than other people's. You hide behind your job title and use your 'position power' to get things done, rather than use the 'personal power' of your influencing skills. You may be predictable and have a low sensitivity to differences between people, which causes you to act in a predictable way. Your presence may make other people uncomfortable.

High score (+20 to +30)

This may mean that you are very willing to adapt to meet the needs of other people. You easily see other people's reasons for doing things. You don't hide behind your job title, but use the 'personal power' of your influencing skills, rather than the power of your position. You can be unpredictable. You spend more time thinking about what makes other people happy than what makes you happy.

Of course life isn't black and white and the above descriptions apply to the two absolute ends of the adaptability scale. Unless you scored +30, think about what I have just said. Look back at your answers to the inventory. Ask yourself the question; ' What can I do to improve my style adaptability?'

Remember

Style adaptability is a skill, which can be learned and developed. Being aware of your preferred style and understanding your style adaptability can help you to develop better relationships.

Three golden rules for successful communications

1   **Person #1 is not person #2 – Treat people as individuals!**
    We are all different and individual. Thank goodness! This might seem to fly in the face of everything we have been discussing about communication style, but it doesn't. What we have learned are some general principles for dealing with people from four 'behavioural' clusters. Life isn't that simple. I'd be insulting you if I tried to pretend that there are only four 'people' in the world. Treat people as individuals.

2   **Person #1 today is different from person #1 yesterday – be sensitive!**

    We all have our moods, both good and bad. We all have our highs and lows. A person who has just returned from an enjoyable holiday may be in a completely different frame of mind from that same person who has been up all night trying to comfort a teething baby! Be sensitive!

3   **'I don't know' is more human than 'I know all the answers'.**

    You will never know *everything* about a person or situation – keep an open-mind. 'I don't know' is more human than 'I know all the answers'.

A friend of mine, whose name is also Malcolm, once summarised what we've discussed in this exercise in a sentence. We had recently moved to Lincolnshire and were keeping our boat at Malcolm's marina. One day, after a relaxing cruise down the river, I was telling him what nice people I'd met on the river, and saying how friendly the people of Lincolnshire are. He said 'You know, people give back what they get'. I think it was a compliment!

CHAPTER TEN

What do you want from your job?

Putting work into perspective

'He that hath a trade hath an estate; he that hath a calling hath an office of profit and honour.'

Benjamin Franklin

Q: Why do you go to work? **A:** To earn a living.

But it goes way beyond that. Money is important – but it isn't everything. Research has shown that, while earnings are important, people expect a good deal more from their jobs. A recent survey by the Industrial Society showed interest/enjoyment, job security and a sense of accomplishment were more important than basic pay for most people. You are not 'most people' though. Study the following job factors and rank them 1, for the factor most important to you, to 15, for the factor least important to you.

Job factor	My importance ranking: 1–15
Advancement opportunities	
Basic pay	
Credit for a job well done	
Flexible hours	
Fully utilising skills/talents	
Go-ahead employer	
Having a say	
Interest/enjoyment	
Job security	
Learning new skills	
Physical working conditions	
Sense of accomplishment	
Skilled management	
Sufficient help/equipment	
Working for a boss you respect	

When you're jobsearching, check to make sure that at least your top five job factors will be satisfied. Don't leap on the salary bandwagon. Yes, it is important but it's not everything.

The grass *may* be greener – but then again it may not. According to an international survey in which 19,000 workers were interviewed, only one out of every three Britons said they enjoy work. The unhappy ones blamed longer hours, commuting time and poor job security for their dissatisfaction. The picture wasn't that different in other industrialised countries with French, German, Russian and Japanese workers expressing a similar level of discontent.

If you're thinking about a career change ask yourself, 'What am I running away from? What am I running towards?'

Imagine you are a personnel manager in a small company. You love the close contact you have with everyone. Your boss, the managing director, trusts and respects the quality of your work and gives you a wide amount of latitude to make decisions. You are given fair appraisals and it is ensured that you're always being stretched a little by involving you in lots of challenging project work. It's also handy having only a 20-minute drive to work. You love your job.

A telephone call from a headhunter, a couple of interviews and you land a job on £3,500 per year more and a company car? Yippee! OK, you'll have to put up with an hour and a half drive into the city each morning. But it's worth it because now you're the specialist in compensation and benefits for 'Huge International' . . . or is it? You're locked in an office on the tenth floor surrounded by computer terminals with a library of policies, procedures and computer printouts. You rarely see your boss. You can do the job standing on your head. You're bored to tears. You're ready to leave after six months, but all of a sudden the jobs have evaporated!

As you identify potential job opportunities, check, as far as you can, that your top five or six job factors will be satisfied – after all, you wouldn't want to be starting all over again in another six months, would you?

Why people resign – the six most common reasons

There are six main reasons why people resign and, usually more than just one of these reasons is involved:

- **Initial expectations mismatch** – the interviewer fails to describe the position accurately. Initial expectations do not match up to the reality of working.
- **Lack of communication** – normal work pressures often make communication difficult. People may feel forgotten, they think they are being given the 'mushroom treatment' – always kept in the dark while up to their waists in manure. Isolation or uncertainty breed insecurity, apathy and cynicism. People resign out of frustration.
- **Challenge** – people hate being in a rut, feeling that they have outgrown their job.
- **Lack of recognition** – how many times have you felt your hard work and commitment have not even been recognised, let alone rewarded?

- **Training and development** – if a person is not developing and being stretched within his or her job, then the company is providing a job rather than a career. Training adds 'value' to the individual. It also makes a person appreciate the company more. It shows the company has a commitment to its people.
- **Culture fit** – every company has its own style or culture. Sometimes there is a mismatch between a person and the company's culture and the employee leaves.

How does your target organisation measure up to these points? Use the following checklist to assess its suitability. If you cannot tick all six, ask yourself if it's the right company for you.

Target organisation checklist

- **Expectations** – do I/they know what I'm/they are letting myself/themselves in for? ☐
- **Communication** – are channels of communication obvious? Do they work? ☐
- **Challenge** – am I going to be stretched? ☐
- **Recognition** – will my contribution be recognised? ☐
- **Training and development** – will I get any? ☐
- **Culture** – do I like their style? Will I fit in? ☐

11

Your work–life balance

Balancing the two

'Occasionally in life there are those moments of unutterable fulfilment which cannot be completely explained by those symbols called words. Their meanings can only be articulated by the inaudible language of the heart.'

Martin Luther King, Jr.

Jobsearching and career planning isn't something you can do in isolation. The decisions you make about your career impact on your life outside work, just as your activities outside work impact on your career, for example business travel is a normal part of organisational life. In considering a new job, you may want to determine how much travel is involved and what effect that will have on your personal and family life. Having to work shifts changes the pattern of people's lives completely.

At the same time, it may be necessary to make certain compromises between your career and personal development. Only you can decide exactly what compromises you are prepared to make.

No matter how challenging and satisfying a job is, it cannot meet all of your needs for personal growth and development. You have a rewarding life outside work as well. Successful people are usually well balanced, with a number of outside interests. A full leisure and family life refreshes them to perform more effectively at work and allows them to bring a broader scope of vision to their jobs.

This chapter helps you to review how well you balance the different areas of your life. You will then set yourself goals for how you want to balance your life in future. The chapter is in three stages – analysing your current work–life balance; deciding where you want the balance to lie; and finally setting some goals and developing a set of actions.

Stage 1

Imagine that the circle in Figure 11.1 is a 'pie' representing your life during the last year. Divide the pie into slices representing how you (or most recently when working) allocate your waking time into the 'slices' of your life. Use any division that is meaningful to you. Possible labels for your slices are:

- attending church
- community and professional activities
- continuing education
- education
- entertainment
- financial management
- fun
- hobbies
- household maintenance
- surfing the Net

- personal development
- professional development
- reading
- relationships
- shopping
- spending time with friends
- sports
- watching TV
- work

The size of each slice should represent the amount of time you spend on each activity. For example, if you spend half your waking hours on work, that should account for half the circle. (Note that you could do stages 1 and 2 using the charting tool of any spreadsheet software you use.)

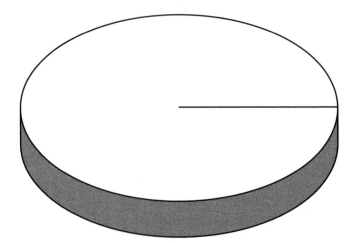

Figure 11.1   Your 'life pie' for the last year

Stage 2

Make a few notes as you answer these questions. Ask yourself:

- Am I satisfied with the way I balance my life?
- What parts are out of balance?
- What is the impact of this neglect on myself and those who are close to me?
- What activities do I spend too much time on and what can I do about it?

Now slice your '*ideal* pie' (in Figure 11.2) as you would like to spend your time. To remind you, possible labels for your slices are:

- attending church
- children
- community and professional activities
- continuing education
- education
- entertainment
- financial management
- fun
- hobbies
- household maintenance
- surfing the Net

- personal development
- physical fitness
- professional development
- reading
- relationships
- shopping
- spending time with friends
- sports
- watching TV
- work

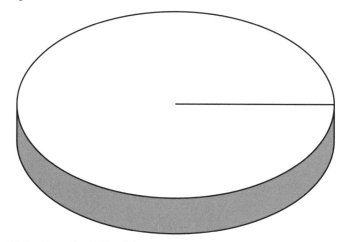

Figure 11.2 Your ideal 'life pie'

Stage 3

Complete the summary and action plan table below. Write your aims in the left-hand column – for example 'I want to become fitter.' In the right-hand column state what you intend to do about your aims – for example 'Join an aerobics club' – to turn your aim into an achievable goal.

Goals and action plan	
Goals	**Action plan: What I'm going to do**
I want to spend more time on:	
I want to spend less time on:	

CHAPTER TWELVE

Your values

What is really important to you in your life?

'For anything worth having one must pay the price; and the price is always work, patience, love, self-sacrifice.'

John Burroughs

Values – what we care about – guide our actions and determine how we experience the world. Values change as we grow older, to reflect experiences and the various stages in our lives and careers. As children, our most important value may be winning the love of our parents. As we grow and mature, new values such as autonomy, achievement and the need of self-approval become important. Parenthood may shift the emphasis once again.

It can be easy to lose touch with what is important to us in the process of managing our day-to-day activities. Also, because many of us do not stop to reflect on our values, we fail to challenge the way we see the world.

Understanding your values can help you in:

- selecting the kind of position and work to suit you
- understanding the kind of people you most like to associate with
- allocating your finances and time to achieve the greatest personal satisfaction.

This exercise will help you to increase your awareness of what is most important to you and what you want out of your life and your career.

- Read the values on the following page. If necessary, modify or rewrite them to make them more meaningful to you – add any values you feel are missing.

● Mark each value in terms of its importance to you as high, medium or low (regardless of how well you are currently satisfying that value in your life). Try to allocate roughly one-third of the values to each category.

Complete the exercise as you think about these values *right now*. And remember, it's not what you think the world wants you to *think*, but what you *value*.

For most people the initial reaction is to place a high ranking on all the values. Try to prioritise what are your most important and least important values at this time in your life.

What I really value in life	Importance		
	High	Medium	Low
Accomplishment – to achieve; to reach the top			
Affection – to obtain and share warmth, caring, companionship with family, friends, colleagues			
Affiliation – to be accepted and liked by others			
Autonomy – to direct my priorities and schedules			
Challenge – to have interesting, challenging work			
Competence – to be respected for my ability			
Expertise – to be a respected authority			
Family – to spend time with my family and to have meaningful relationships			
Growth – to maximise my full potential; to be constantly learning, changing and developing			
Health – physical health, fitness			
Integrity – to have the courage of my convictions; to be honest, to uphold my beliefs			
Leadership – to influence and direct others			
Location – to live where I want to live			
Money – to be financially successful			
Pleasure – to have fun; to enjoy life and work			
Recognition – to have status and the respect of others			
Security – to achieve a secure financial situation			
Service – to help other people; to contribute to the well being of others; to help improve society			
Spiritual – inner harmony; to be at peace with myself and live by my moral and ethical beliefs			
Other values –			

Summarising your values

Now analyse how your values are currently being satisfied and what you must do in the future. You'll probably find that some trends have emerged and that you want to combine two, three or four values into one statement.

At this time in my life my five most important values are:

1 _____ 2 _____ 3 _____ 4 _____ 5 _____

Values which must be satisfied in my:

Working life	Personal life

Ways in which I may be able to achieve greater satisfaction of my values in my working life are:

_____

_____

_____

_____

Ways in which I may be able to achieve greater satisfaction of my values in my personal life are:

_____

_____

_____

_____

CHAPTER THIRTEEN

Your life's achievements

Sing your own praises

'They are able because they think they are able.'

Virgil

Do you keep a 'brag box', as my friend Tony calls it? My own is a bursting box file . . . and as I'm writing this, I'm reminding myself that it is overdue for updating! I can't think of a better name than the one Tony uses, so we'll call it a brag box! I'm talking about a collection point for documents logging your achievements through life.

When you come to complete your CV, or find you've got just one hour to fill in an application form in order to catch the post, you'll be glad of your brag box!

Do you keep a brag box?

Some of the things to include in your brag box (either as copies or originals) could be:

- Birth certificate
- Exam certificates
- Marriage certificate
- Children's birth certificates
- Passport (for number)
- Driving licence
- Membership certificates for professional institutes
- Licences to practise
- Career evaluations
- Testimonials
- Appraisals
- CPD (continuous professional development) file
- Degree(s)
- Examples of your work
- CV
- Personality and other evaluations
- Historical salary data
- Performance rankings, e.g. sales figures
- Special thank-you letter from your boss or the MD!
- Sports certificates
- This book!

As well as the functional aspect, you'll find your brag box useful for cheering you up on a wet Tuesday afternoon, when you feel as if you've telephoned everyone in the world and 'They're all in meetings'! But don't get too lost down memory lane . . . the meetings do end!

If you haven't got a brag box start one now!

Putting your brag box to work

Identifying your achievements will help you to realise that you have a wide variety of skills. You can use the information you develop in this exercise in CV presentation, completion of application forms and in preparing for job interviews.

Use the information in your brag box to help you to identify achievements you are proud of. Pick:

- four from the past two years
- three from the five-year period before that.

Now think about the skills you used and what made your achievements so satisfying. The following phrases are often used in describing achievements.

Work achievements

Improved productivity in _____ by _____

Successfully convinced (my manager, subordinates, etc.) to_____

Developed (introduced, designed, etc.) a new (method/system, etc.)

for_____ resulting in _____

Motivated subordinates by _____

Detected a serious error in (a procedure, filing system, report, etc.)

and_____ .

Improved technological process (service etc.) by_____

Successfully arranged and ran a meeting on _____

Changed _____

Improved quality control in _____ by _____

Successfully arranged and ran a meeting on _____

Initiated and implemented a (programme campaign, process, etc.)

to_____

Increased market share of _____

Non-work achievements

Created (managed, ran, etc.) a fund-raising campaign for (name of charitable, athletic or artistic activity/group).

Successfully counselled, advised, helped a friend to _____

Organised (coordinated etc.) a charitable drive for _____

Established (acted as secretary of) a professional association (social, athletic club, etc.)_____

Acted as a member of a committee or chaired a committee. _____

As (a founding member of a local organisation) created a campaign

to_____ , successfully raised funds for_____ etc.

Organised a day trip to_____ for a group of_____ (mothers and toddlers).

Did (oversaw) the decorations for _____

Successfully renovated my house myself_____

Having identified your achievements, complete the tables on the following pages – the first is an example to help you to start the process.

Achievement	Skills used	What made the achievement satisfying?
Co-ordinated sponsored run	Conceived the campaign	Managing
Enlisted six volunteers to assist in organising the campaign	Managing others	Planning the campaign
	Motivating others	Running meetings
Informed local newspaper to generate publicity	Planning	Contributing to something I believe in
	Organising	The results – £5000!
Ran four meetings with volunteers	Delegating tasks	Being recognised
	Running effective meetings	Being in the limelight
Coordinated the volunteers by assigning tasks	Public relations – selling the campaign	
Developed plan to go to the schools to inform people about the run and enlist volunteers	Persuading people to participate	
Got 200 people to take part in the run		

Achievements from the past two years		
Achievement	**Skills used**	**What made the achievement satisfying?**

Achievements from the past seven years		
Achievement	**Skills used**	**What made the achievement satisfying?**

CHAPTER FOURTEEN

Getting feedback from others

Developing a balanced view of yourself

'O wad some Pow'r the giftie gie us
To see oursels as others see us!
It wad frae mony a blunder free us,
And foolish notion.'

Robert Burns

All the exercises so far have concentrated on self-analysis. The next step is to gather information about how other people see you. No matter how honest and thoughtful you have been, we all have blind spots! Others may point to weaknesses we are unaware of or, more commonly, strengths and abilities we have underestimated.

Clearly, no two people will see you in exactly the same way. Neither is it true that other people will always see you more accurately than you see yourself. By talking to people whose opinion you value, you will develop a clearer picture of yourself.

Whose opinion do I value?

Write down the names of people whose opinions you value. These may be your:

- current manager
- colleagues
- friends
- partner

- previous manager
- subordinates
- family members
- neighbours

Ideally they:

- have seen you in different situations
- know you well and how you react to different situations
- have your best interests at heart
- are perceptive.

People whose opinions I value:

What sort of feedback do you want?

The feedback you get from each person will, of course, depend on your relationship with them.

Friends and family can provide you with important feedback in such areas as your interpersonal skills, decision-making style, communication skills, ease of social interaction, some of your personality characteristics, how well you plan; how well organised you are, etc.

Don't discount this feedback. If you can do something well at a party or at home, then the chances are that you can also do it well at work. Similarly, weaknesses seen at home are probably applicable to work as well. For example, if your partner tells you that you don't listen very well or that you have difficulties managing your temper, then you probably have similar difficulties in the work environment!

Your manager and other work contacts (current or past) are obviously an important source of information. Some questions you may want to ask are:

- What do you see as my major skills? Strengths?
- What do you see as my major development areas?
- How can I improve how I am seen by others?

- What areas should I try to improve ?
- What kinds of job do you think I can realistically aspire to over the next few years?
- Are you aware of any jobs that I would do well?
- How realistic do you think my career goals are, based on what I've told you?
- What training and/or development do you think I need to attain these goals?
- What are the possible obstacles to me accomplishing the goals?
- What do you see as the key things I could do to improve my chances of achieving the goals?

Remember, people like to be asked for their opinions. Some may surprise you with their honesty and openness.

Be prepared to feel a little down when they talk to you about your limitations, and be prepared for the red glow of embarrassment which will come when they start to sing your praises!

If the people you have asked are unused to giving this sort of feedback, they may appreciate some notice of your questions. In addition, giving them a copy of the page from the next chapter 'Get a coach' will help.

Based on the feedback you have received you may wish to develop new skills and abilities. This may be particularly relevant if you're returning to work after a break, for example bringing up a family, looking after an elderly relative or after a spell in full-time education. Some ways of doing this are:

- working with someone
- taking a training course
- continuing your education
- taking a developmental assignment
- enlarging your position by taking on responsibilities that will stretch you
- joining a club or society, especially as a committee member
- reading.

Clearly some of the options above are only available to people currently in work. If you aren't, think laterally to try to identify alternatives, for example work placement with a local employer.

Now try to identify some new skills and think about their development.

If you were to develop new skills and abilities:

What skills, knowledge or abilities do you want to develop?

_____

_____

_____

_____

How will you do this?

_____

_____

_____

_____

In what ways might you want to develop yourself?

_____

_____

_____

_____

How can you do that?

_____

_____

_____

_____

CHAPTER FIFTEEN

Get a coach

A 'sounding board' for your ideas

'There is no such thing as a "self-made" man. We are made up of thousands of others. Everyone who has ever done a kind deed for us, or spoken one word of encouragement to us, has entered into the make-up of our character and of our thoughts, as well as our success.'

George Matthew Adams

Do you have someone you can use as a sounding board for your ideas? As you develop your career, life, jobsearching ideas and plans, you will find it very beneficial to 'bounce' them off someone else. They'll be far more meaningful when you explain them to someone else. If you have access to a professional career coach, a counsellor or careers adviser then I'm sure you'll find their help invaluable. If you haven't then don't despair, all is not lost.

Who should you ask?

What about a favourite uncle or aunt? An old school/college/university friend? A current or previous work colleague? A neighbour? A fellow member of a sports or social club? Ask someone who knows you well and whose opinion you value. You will probably find it best not to use your partner. Please don't misunderstand me – I'm not advising that you should exclude your partner; not at all. But they may not be able to 'see the wood for the trees' because of their emotional involvement.

What qualities should a coach have?

- A coach should be a good listener – you should do most of the talking.
- A coach should have a genuine interest in you.
- There should be mutual respect as it is important that you talk as equals.
- A coach should be in touch with reality – if your dreams and goals become unrealistic the coach should help you back to earth gently.

Remember, your coach is not your adviser. A good coach won't begin sentences with 'If I were you I would . . .' or 'Why don't you . . .?'. It's your job to develop the ideas and use your coach as a 'testing ground'.

A simple test to see if they are the right person can be to ask yourself, 'Would I choose this person as my boss?'

When should you meet?

It is a good idea to have regular meetings for an hour or so weekly or fortnightly. Failing that you can exchange e-mails, text messages or keep in touch by phone.

What are the benefits?

You will find that your plans are modified, refined and become more realistic. And all it will cost you is a box of chocolates, a special thank-you at Christmas or a couple of beers!

You may wish to give a photocopy of the next page to your coach.

Selecting a coach – giving feedback

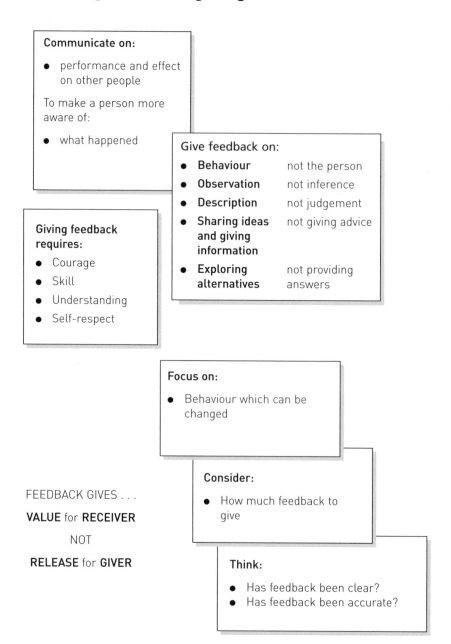

Communicate on:

- performance and effect on other people

To make a person more aware of:

- what happened

Give feedback on:

- **Behaviour**   not the person
- **Observation**   not inference
- **Description**   not judgement
- **Sharing ideas and giving information**   not giving advice
- **Exploring alternatives**   not providing answers

Giving feedback requires:

- Courage
- Skill
- Understanding
- Self-respect

Focus on:

- Behaviour which can be changed

FEEDBACK GIVES . . .

VALUE for **RECEIVER**

NOT

RELEASE for **GIVER**

Consider:

- How much feedback to give

Think:

- Has feedback been clear?
- Has feedback been accurate?

STEP TWO

Where are you going?

A new direction

'There is only one success – to be able to spend your life in your way.'

Christopher Morley

Before we begin

Wouldn't it be wonderful if you could work through a few exercises to help you know more about yourself, decide on a new career direction, pick up the newspaper, make a few phone calls and, hey presto, get a new job!

Unfortunately life isn't like that.

So far in this book the principal point of focus has been you. But you don't live your life in a vacuum. The job you want is out there in the real world.

We are now going to switch to a wider view. *You* will still be a major part of the picture and we will start to use some of the things you have learned about yourself in Step 1.

We will also consider the external environment – what jobs could you do? What are good bets for the future and the not so good bets?

I'm not going to offer you a list of jobs though. If I did there wouldn't be space for anything else in the book! Indeed, we would need an extra 20 or 30 volumes. Through your research activities *you* will identify job opportunities. Many of which you haven't even thought of so far!

To put it into context, most organisations write a business plan to help them to analyse their current situation, and to plan what they are going to do for the future. As a career and life planner you are the managing director of 'The Me Corporation' so in this section we'll develop your 'business plan'.

CHAPTER SIXTEEN

Your new direction

Identifying and evaluating new options

'A state without the means of some change is without the means of its conservation.'

Edmund Burke

This chapter uses a really powerful technique to bring together the information you have built up about yourself in the earlier exercises and put them into the context of the 'outside world' – the external environment. When you have done this, you can set your course for your new direction.

A technique used widely in business to help in evaluating situations is SWOT analysis. SWOT stands for:

- Strengths
- Weaknesses
- Opportunities
- Threats

You may have come across the SWOT analysis technique at work, or even used it to analyse business situations.

SWOT analysis can be an extremely useful technique in thinking about what you can offer relative to your external environment, i.e. the job market. SWOT analysis helps you to take stock of your position so that you can plan what you want to do next.

The strengths and weaknesses elements are personal to you. Opportunities and threats lie in the external environment.

Use the format on the following pages to build up your own SWOT analysis. It can be helpful if you gather all the information on a 'big scale' – like using a sheet of flipchart paper or four pieces of A3 paper spread across the kitchen table! It may take a few days to do a complete analysis, so do some work on it and keep coming back to it. Don't be in too much of a rush!

Use your SWOT analysis to:

- identify how you can maximise the use of your strengths
- see how you can compensate for your weaknesses
- identify opportunities, particularly those which may not be immediately obvious
- if at all possible see if threats can be turned into opportunities.

My experience of using this technique, on dozens of occasions, is that when you gather all the information like this, ideas that you'd never had before will start to 'leap out of the paper'. Two heads are better than one – why not get also some input from friends/family/colleagues, etc?

The first part of the exercise (strengths and weaknesses) should be straightforward, especially if you have completed the earlier exercises in 'Step 1'. Opportunities and threats may be more difficult to identify so here are a few examples.

- **Opportunities** – as society changes and technology advances, new jobs emerge – 'conveyancing' shops no longer need a qualified solicitor; computers need systems analysts/programmers/operators; the Internet allows people to work in different locations, many even telecommute and do business with people at the other side of the world in split-seconds; new prisons are opening with 'contracted' staff; people are becoming more environmentally conscious; 'fringe' medicine is becoming more acceptable; people are becoming more aware of their health and fitness. These, and many others, are areas where new jobs are emerging.
- **Threats** – these are the external barriers to you achieving your career goals – like the closure of a major company in your area. Try to see if external threats can be turned into opportunities. This might seem to be an insurmountable challenge, but it can sometimes be done. For example Diane, a friend of mine, wanted to return to work as a teacher after

starting a family. The external 'threat' to her doing this was that there was no suitable childcare available. If Diane and Keith, her husband, were having difficulty finding nursery places then surely other parents would be having the same problem? Their answer was to start a daycare nursery. Now, in addition to Diane's job as a teacher and Keith's as a college lecturer, they jointly run a nursery employing four people.

My swot analysis	
In my close environment	
S – my personal strengths	W – my personal weaknesses
In my external environment	
O – opportunities	T – threats

Evaluating your swot analysis

Your SWOT analysis won't provide an instant and magic answer but, as I said earlier, in my experience it seems that ideas jump out of the pages when you look at all four factors side-by-side.

If you are having difficulty coming up with ideas, then the next exercise should help you.

Research time – job ideas

Even with Internet access, if you try to do this exercise anywhere other than in your local library (where you have access to directories, careers brochures and a hundred and one sources of valuable information) you won't even scratch the surface.

Take yourself off to the library

Take yourself off to the library and ask the librarian to advise on suitable references both in the 'industry and organisations' and the 'careers' sections. Alternatively, go to your local careers office – they aren't just for school leavers. The staff are incredibly helpful people and some will even start to act as your research assistants, if you explain what you are doing and ask for their advice in the right way! Many of them also have free access to the Internet where there are thousands of career sites. If you're new to searching the Net careers office staff can help you to find your way around – if you ask.

Don't be in too much of a hurry. Brainstorm ideas with your partner and friends. Research isn't a 'do it' once and you're finished process either. Keep coming back to this section to add new ideas and to give you inspiration.

Use the tables on the next two pages to collect your thoughts.

Job ideas 1

My ideal job will provide the following.

Uses for my skills and knowledge	Responsibilities
Working conditions and locality	Salary/benefits package
Interpersonal environment	Opportunities

Job ideas 2

Write down the names of companies, government bodies, charitable organisations, etc. where you may be able to find your ideal job – use the library, friends, the Internet, networking contacts and yourself as resources.

Job ideas 3

Write down the names of jobs you could do.

Decision-making time!

After you have invested time and effort in the 'job ideas' exercise, you will arrive at a vast number of options – especially when you combine the different jobs and the different potential workplaces.

If you had an army of secretaries and researchers working for you, then you could allocate tasks and blitz every possibility straight away. The reality of life is that you are probably on your own, so you need to set priorities so that you can direct your energies in the right direction.

Now try to prioritise the options available to you so that you arrive at your top *five* priority targets. Your 'priority classification criteria' are the things identified in the job ideas 1 exercise. It's very rare that only one job will satisfy all of a person's 'ideal' criteria and the same person might identify their five top priority jobs as, for example:

- an assistant brand manager in a large company
- a market research executive in an agency
- an advertising agency account executive
- a market research manager in a large company
- a brand manager in a small- or medium-sized company.

The only judge of the importance of each of your 'ideal' factors is you. Now write your five target jobs below.

Job idea 1 _____

Job idea 2 _____

Job idea 3 _____

Job idea 4 _____

Job idea 5 _____

Targeting

Having identified your priorities, you still need to identify your top priority so that you can really target your jobsearch.

If you make your jobsearch too vague, then you will confuse people in your network – potential employers and recruitment consultants. Which of the above five job options is your number one target, or is it difficult to choose?

People use many different decision-making methods. A technique I have found useful is 'force-field analysis'. Quite simply, you write the pros and cons of making a decision alongside each other in lists. When you have collected all the pros and cons you allocate an arbitrary 'weighting', out of 10, to each point – only you can be the judge. Using force-field analysis takes only a few minutes and can really help in making a decision. Try it!

When you evaluate each of your five options using force-field analysis, the one with the highest score when you have subtracted the 'restraining forces' column from the 'active forces' column is the one you should go for as a first priority.

As an example look at the force-field analysis in Table 16.1 – it is the one I used to help me to decide whether or not to start my own business.

Table 16.1 Force-field analysis example

Active forces + positives Why should I go for this option?	Score (max. 10)	Restraining forces – Negatives What's holding me back?	Score (max 10)
Master of my own destiny	10	Lack of predictable income	6
Earnings potential	7	Long-term security	5
Variety	7	Away from home?	5
Government aid/advice	5	Lack of permanence	3
		Need office	2
Redundancy package		Health insurance/	
available	8	life assurance	2
I can set company's direction	8	Pension	3
I am able to work alone	7	Lack of challenge from peers	5
Market exists	7	Collection of revenue	5
Resources (me + support)	9	Ability to obtain mortgage	5
		Not seeing job through	5
		No income	2
Total +	68	Total –	48

Even though there were *more* negative reasons than positive, the *strength* of the positive argument won!

Using your Priority 1 target, evaluate your options using Table 16.2.

As you start to exhaust the possibilities for your number one target move to number two, and so on.

Table 16.2 Priority 1 target

Active forces + positives Why should I go for this option?	Score (max. 10)	Restraining forces – Negatives What's holding me back?	Score (max 10)
Total +		Total –	

Targeting your jobsearch gives you a clear direction to move in, just like having a well-printed map.

CHAPTER SEVENTEEN

Setting your goals

Setting long- and short-term goals

'When I was young I observed that nine out of every ten things I did were failures, so I did ten times more work.'

George Bernard Shaw

Why is goal setting important?

'A goal is a dream taken seriously'. Put another way, from *South Pacific*; '*You've got to have a dream, if you don't have a dream, how you going to have a dream come true?*' In this chapter we will formalise your dreams about the future into goals.

Goal setting gives you a target to aim for. Organisations and businesses constantly use goal setting to help them to achieve things such as production and sales targets. Similarly, many successful people say that an element of their success is due to goal setting. Goals are specific – 'to be happy' is not a goal, it is an aim. Achieving goals is the process of putting one foot after the other, along the stepping stones that lead to happiness. A good test of a goal is to see if it is **SMART:**

- **Specific** – for example, if it is to get a job then list the title, type of organisation, etc.
- **Measurable** – what criteria will you use to measure your achievement?
- **Achievable** – you will become demotivated if you fail to achieve your goal – but don't make it too easy, make it challenging.
- **Relevant** – goals should relate to what you want to achieve directly.
- **Timed** – set a target completion date.

An example of a jobsearcher's goals could be 'Each day next week I will make contact with a minimum of three people on my network list and will get two more names from each of them.'

A longer term goal might be 'Within four months I will get a job as a development engineer, in a medium/large electronics company, within 30 miles of home, on £X000 per year.'

I know they sound a bit wordy but 'I'm going to make some phone calls and I'm going to get a job in electronics' just aren't goals. Goals state what you need to *do* to reach your aims.

Goals can be short- or long-term and relate to all aspects of life. Use Table 17.1 to help you to set your goals. Set the long-term goals first, then your short-term goals. Use everything you have learned from the previous exercises to help you to set your career and life goals. In this exercise you really are 'nailing your colours to your mast' (see Chapter 1).

Table 17.1 My career and life goals

Personal contract:
I am going to achieve the following career and life goals in
the next five years

GOALS	Home and family	Work	Social and community	Self (leisure, study etc.)
	6 months	6 months	6 months	6 months
Goal 1				
Goal 2				
Goal 3				
	1 year	1 year	1 year	1 year
Goal 1				
Goal 2				
	2 years	2 years	2 years	2 years
Goal 1				
Goal 2				
	5 years	5 years	5 years	5 years
Goal 1				
Goal 2				

Signature:..

Date: ....

Make a note of what you might need to do to resolve any conflicts

_____

_____

_____

_____

The following chart shows how you can turn goals into strategies and actions.

Term	Definition	A personal example
Mission	Overriding premise in line with your values or expectations	_Be healthy and look good_
Aim	General statement of aim or purpose	_Lose weight_
Goal	Quantification (if possible) or more precise statement of the goal	_Lose five kilos by Christmas_
Strategies	Broad categories or types of action to achieve objectives	_Diet and exercise_
Actions/tasks/ tactics	Individual steps to implement strategies	_Eliminate desserts/snacks/butter. Limit alcohol. Exercise every day_

CHAPTER EIGHTEEN

Creating your own job

Working for yourself; interim, consulting and portfolio working

'Diligence is the mother of good luck'.

Benjamin Franklin

Working for yourself

When I wrote the first edition of this book in 1993, my aim was to advise people on how to get a 'normal' job with a wage or salary. Since then the world of work has changed and more and more people are moving into generating an income by creating their own work, either by running a business, working as a freelancer or being a portfolio worker.

The rate of new business start-ups is higher than ever – 400,000 a year. Could you be next? Let's consider some of the pros and cons of creating your own job.

On one side of the equation there's the chance that your earnings will be lower than you anticipate. Your working hours may well be longer than you have ever worked before and you could stretch your personal relationships to their limits, or maybe even beyond.

On the other side there is a multitude of positives. If you're self-employed there will be no cap on your potential earnings, and many people do earn considerably more than they had done previously. You'll 'call the shots' – if you want time off work for a day trip to the seaside, you won't have to fill in a holiday request form and then wait for approval. You just do it! And as for relationships there's a great opportunity for jointly sharing, and participating in something that you 'own', with your partner.

While some people start their own business in the search for fame or fortune, or both, the main driver for 'going it alone' seems to be 'freedom'. When you create your own job you have more control over your life. You have freedom to choose the kind of work you do, freedom to choose your working hours, freedom to set your earnings target, freedom . . . Clearly it isn't for everybody, and it isn't a decision to be taken lightly, but for some people it really is the best thing they ever did. I know it was one of the best decisions I have ever made in my life!

If it is for you, then there are a number of ways you can move into self-employment. You can buy an existing business, for example a guest house. It has an established trading record and can be running and generating an income from day one. Or you can start your own guest house and hope that people will come to stay with you. Or you could buy a franchise and pay a large sum of money upfront for anything from a fast-food restaurant to a carpet cleaning company.

Now for a reality check – most new business ventures fail! I haven't said that to be negative, but whenever you read about new business start-ups you'll find that there is a very high failure rate. Conversely there is a very high success rate with franchises. One consideration when starting a business should be whether you want it to provide you with only a 'here and now' income, or whether you also want to build a business that you can sell when you retire. If you want to get a flavour of the huge diversity of business options available for self-employment, buy a copy of *Daltons Weekly* from your newsagent or have a look at their website, *www.daltons.co.uk*.

If you're considering self-employment you'll increase your chances of success by thoroughly researching and planning your business idea. Make sure that you integrate your career and life goals into your business plan. Tell yourself that you can and will succeed! When I started out on my own 15 years ago, I never entertained the idea that my business might fail! Some (negative thinkers) would have said that I was naïve. I prefer to say that I have a positive mental attitude. Remember – 'the glass is always full' (see Chapter 1).

Gather as much information as you can. The Department of Employment has an excellent induction scheme for new business start-ups (details from your local job centre). The high street banks produce free information packs (the NatWest is very useful). Contact your local Business Link for free courses and information packs.

Read as many books as you can on self-employment. I can heartily recommend *From Acorns – how to build your brilliant business from scratch* by Caspian Woods, *Start Your Business Week by Week* by Steve Parks and *The White Ladder Diaries* by Ros Jay (a personal account of starting a small business).

Talk to as many people as you can who run their own businesses – your friendly fish and chip shop owner; local landlord, newsagent, etc. No matter what the business, the potential problems are usually the same – cash flow, marketing, obtaining supplies. With the greatest of respect to college lecturers, career counsellors and coaches, you'll find out what it's really like by talking to self-employed people. You'll also hear, no doubt, of the enormous satisfaction that comes from being self-employed. But I don't want to oversell.

Research, research, research – and be wary of others. Partnerships, even among 'best friends', often collapse because of disagreements. As I said earlier, the figures show that the majority of new businesses fail. You may be able to reduce the risk by buying a franchise, but even franchises fail. I know this from the bitter experience of having lost over £30,000, and as much again in other ways, on a franchise. I was lied to when the person sold me the franchise. But I could have avoided my losses and walked away from the 'opportunity' if I had researched the company more thoroughly. I should have talked to many, many more people. Learn from my mistake. Ask to see audited accounts, ask to speak to suppliers, ask to see actual sales figures and profits, ask to speak to satisfied customers, ask the person who's selling you the franchise to produce factual evidence of their previous successes. If anything doesn't look right, then walk away. There are plenty more fish in the sea. The financial and psychological scars from my experience will take many years to heal.

Most important of all, talk your idea through with your partner (if you have one) – such support is essential.

If, when you have gathered all of the information, you remain totally committed to it then abandon your jobsearch (you cannot do either of them half-heartedly) and . . . go for it. And good luck!

There are some useful resources for going it alone at: *www.bt.com/getstarted.*

Freelancing, consulting and interim work

For many people interim working, freelancing, consulting or becoming part of the 'talent market' gives the freedom from having a 'real job' without the risk of setting off in a completely different direction and starting a new business.

Outsourcing – a new work paradigm

Years ago, 'consultant' was a word that many executives put on their CV to cover a period of unemployment. The world is now very different. Many organisations have taken the decision to concentrate on their 'core' business and to 'outsource', or buy in, expertise as needed. Improvements in employee rights and the rising cost of making staff redundant also mean that organisations are very wary of increasing headcount if they can avoid it. This creates a phenomenal number of opportunities for people who can be contracted in for short periods. Some people, especially in skill shortage areas, keep busy through temporary work and interim management assignments gained through employment agencies. If this kind of lifestyle appeals to you then start contacting recruitment agencies that specialise in 'temp' and 'interim assignments' and build a relationship with a small select number.

I could write a whole book on the dos and dont's of consulting (now there's an idea!). If you're considering going it alone as a freelancer, or consultant here's a starting point.

Starting out as a freelancer/consultant

Four keys to success

- *Your vision of what success means to you* – what are you hoping to achieve for yourself?

- **Your skill and knowledge set** – what have you got that people will want to buy in? How will you add value to your customer's organisation?
- **Generate revenue** – communication: marketing and selling. How will people learn who you are and then make the decision to use you?
- **Control costs** – budgeting and cash flow control.

Action plan

Don't talk to potential customers until you have done all of the following.

- Established your vision of what success means to you. It took me nearly a month when I first started out.
- Convinced yourself that you've got something to offer. If you can't convince yourself, then how will you convince a customer?
- Clarified what you're offering. When I first started out I made the mistake of trying to offer too much. Potential customers were confused. When I focused on one area of expertise, training and development, business took off.
- Established that the market exists. Do your market research (OK you'll need to talk to potential customers to do this, but remember, you're in asking mode).
- Prepared a business plan and a marketing plan.
- Prepared a budget and a cash flow forecast (guidelines and even free software are available from your friendly bank manager).
- Decided what you're going to charge. Which sector of the market? Aldi, Lidl, Kwik Save, Asda/Wal-Mart, Tesco, Marks & Spencer, Waitrose, Harrods and Fortnum and Mason all sell groceries, but their products and prices are targeted at different market sectors.
- Picked your professional advisers. My bookkeeper and my accountant are both freelancers and have been with me for almost a decade.
- Chosen a name for your business and got a URL (website address). You may find it easier to check what website names are available, and then choose your trading name. Try *www.easyspace.com* to find if your website is available or *www.nominet.org.uk* if you want to learn more about registering a UK website.

- Established how you're going to finance the start-up. Even if you can do it on a shoestring and you can win some business in your first week, it may be weeks or even months, before the payments start to roll in.

- Set up your office. I know hot-desking (last one into the office gets the cleaner's cupboard) and 'virtual offices' (have laptop and mobile phone, will consult) are becoming popular, but I'm a bit old-fashioned and I like to have my own office space.

- Talked to your tax office.

- Talked to a financial planning adviser about insurance, such as office contents and vehicle, pensions, professional indemnity and public liability.

- Got free advice on start-ups from your local Business Link.

- Set up customer records and systems, such as credit and invoicing procedures. Establish your trading terms and conditions and draw up model contracts. All pretty boring stuff, but essential if you are going to be taken seriously. Fortunately there's lots of good, inexpensive software around to guide you through the maze.

By all means produce a nice logo and some product literature, but I can't emphasise too much the importance of networking when working as a 'freelancer'. I started working as a consultant in 1990. Since then, I'd say that 90 per cent of the work that I have got has been through personal contacts (better re-read the section on networking!).

Portfolio working

The days of the gold watch for long service are long gone. Most people will have half a dozen careers by the time they retire. Many people are 'breaking the mould' of a traditional 9–5 workday by replacing / supplementing their income from a portfolio of other 'jobs'. Can you really earn a fortune on the Internet? Are you a budding property developer? What are the other options? Is the flexible income lifestyle for you

Portfolio working is a 'new age' expression for having a number of 'income streams'. If you get bored doing the same job every day, need to supplement your pension, have found it to be just impossible to get a 'real' job in spite of all your efforts, want to supplement the earnings from a regular job or just want to keep yourself from being bored in retirement then portfolio working may be for you. Here are some portfolio workers that I know.

- Brian retired in his early fifties after a career in the army and wanted to supplement his pension. He's a keen gardener and a good DIY'er and so he placed a few cards in local newsagents offering his service maintaining gardens and doing household repairs. In no time at all he had a client base of mainly retired people who needed a bit of extra help. He's now got more work than he needs and a waiting list of clients.

- Susan divides her time between working as a freelance trainer, writing magazine articles and painting pictures, which she sells in a local gallery.

- Brian is a safety manager on an oil rig and Christine has a small antiques shop. They used their savings to buy an investment property and now have a regular income from renting it to students. They also buy properties at auction, which they develop and decorate using professional tradespeople, and then sell on at a profit.

- Bob is retired and buys job lots of more or less anything at auctions, which he then sells at car boot sales.

- Bill and Doreen are retired but are far too active to stop working, so they run their home as a B&B. Bill also buys antique furniture at auctions, which he then restores and sells on at auctions at a profit.

- Kathleen is a skilled secretary and seamstress. She works as a part-time secretary and earns a significant additional income by making curtains and other soft-furnishings.

There's nothing new about people having a number of jobs, but there's a new respectability emerging of having a 'number of irons in the fire' and being a portfolio worker. There are hundreds of options available for generating an income, from delivering pizzas to selling insurance. Here are three that might be worth exploring.

- **Internet auction sales** – there are a number of sites, but the market leader by far is eBay. I have to confess to being something of an eBay addict as a seller and a buyer. I got hooked a number of years ago when we moved house and I cleared out the loft. My wife and I are pathological hoarders and we go through phases of 'simplifying our lives' using eBay. Since I first joined I've achieved a rating of over 750 and have become a Powerseller – no you don't get a leotard and a cape! If you enjoy 'wheeling and dealing' and have basic computer skills then you could easily supplement your income this way. But beware of the stories you read in the press of people earning fortunes. For every one of them there are thousands making respectable, but modest, amounts. The downside is that it takes a lot more time than you can imagine to photograph items, write descriptions, upload the information and answer questions. The commissions and money handling fees can cut big slices out of your profits. And it can take ages to pack and ship items – and packages do go missing. All of that said, you can sell to an international audience and you can achieve prices that you never imagined possible! I advertised my old company car twice in the local newspaper and didn't get one phone call. I advertised it on eBay and sold it for £500 more than I'd asked in the paper! Everything you need to know about selling on eBay is right there on *www.ebay.co.uk*.

- **Mr/Ms Fixit** – can you wallpaper a room? Paint window frames? Make a pair of curtains? Mow a lawn? Fit a new kitchen? Clean a house so that it shines like a new pin? Do any of the multitude of practical things that are needed to keep a home in order? There's probably a market for your skills right on your doorstep. Why? Well, there are a number of reasons. First we have a huge deficit of professionally qualified people with practical skills – plumbers, joiners, painters and decorators etc. Second there are generations of people who have been/are going through school without learning the carpentry/metalworking/domestic science skills that were taught in schools two or three decades ago. Finally the population is ageing. As people get older, even with the best will in the world, they become less able to do the household jobs that require stamina and fitness or manual dexterity. I can almost guarantee that if, like Brian I mentioned earlier, you place a few cards in the local newsagents and do a good job for a few people at a fair price, then you'll have a trail of people beating a path to your door and a steady income.

- **Internet teleworking** – where do I begin? There are so, so many things that can be done using computers and the Internet. You can do the work in the comfort of your own home for customers in the next village or twelve thousand miles away. You can write articles, write computer games, design brochures, edit a magazine, design a website, create artwork, compose music, create a set of accounts. There are thousands of work opportunities out there on the Net. Just do a search on Google for your particular expertise and you'll see what I mean. But beware, there are hundreds of 'clubs' on the Internet for every kind of freelancer. Many of them will provide work for you, but many won't. They'll hook you with an offer of an initial free membership and then charge you a small monthly subscription, rather than an annual fee. Once you've signed up it's easy to forget that you're making the payment – after two or three months ask yourself if you're getting value for money. How can you guarantee that you will be paid for your work? Tread warily. Once you've sent the work you can't get it back. If your client is in another country you may have little or no protection if you don't get paid. I hope I haven't sounded negative, but it really is humiliating to do a big chunk of work only to find that you'll never get paid for it. Check things out and establish mutually beneficial working relationships with your clients and you can generate a comfortable income without leaving home. What's more, you can wear your slippers to work, have the dog by your side and stop for a cuppa when you want to!

If you want to read more about the emerging flexible working life I can recommend 'Jobshift: how to prosper in a workplace without jobs' and also 'Creating You & Co.: learn to think like the CEO of your own career', both by William Bridges.

How will you get there?

How to get the job you want

'The three great essentials to achieve anything worthwhile are first, hard work; second, stick-to-it-iveness; third, common sense.'

Thomas A. Edison

Before we begin

This section is devoted to the tactics of getting a job. Think of each of the exercises as a different skill of a craftsperson – you. The exercises are the tools to help you to get your new job.

There is no 'one right way' to get a job and the application and selection process can vary from less than one hour to many months.

Work on those exercises which will help you to develop those skills which you need to help you to get the job you want.

CHAPTER NINETEEN

Managing your jobsearch

Project and time management skills

'Lost yesterday, somewhere between sunrise and sunset, two golden hours, each set with sixty diamond minutes. No reward is offered, they are gone for ever.'

Horace Mann

If you're currently working and also jobsearching then you have a challenging job balancing your time between the two. If your current full-time occupation is jobsearching then the apparent lack of structure can be daunting. It can scare some people into doing anything – that bit of decorating I've been putting off, or a visit to long lost friends – anything other than jobsearching. The answer to both is to have planning and control systems.

Organise yourself and manage your time

Jobsearching is a job.

- Allocate some 'office space' at home where you can work undisturbed. If you haven't got one, then buy, beg or borrow a PC with a good printer. Don't be put off by thinking that you have to have the latest 'all singing and dancing' PC. You only need something fairly basic if you're surfing the Net for jobs and for word-processing. You can pick up a bargain from the newspaper or one of the Internet auction sites, such as eBay.

- Keep a diary and use it for both planning your time and for recording appointments.

- In addition to the files on your hard disk, have a paper-based filing system using files, box files or ring binders.

- Work expands to fill the time available – set deadlines for each task.

- Set daily objectives – use the daily action planner on page 131 and stick to it.

- Prioritise the day's tasks – A: must; B: should; C: could. Only move to the Bs when the As are finished, and to the Cs when the Bs are finished. Don't do the Cs first just because they can be done quickly. Subdivide As into A1, A2, A3, and do A1 first!

- Block off times in your diary for different parts of your jobsearch.

- Decide when you are at your best for doing things, for example best at telephoning early morning, good at planning early evening.

- Plan for tomorrow at the end of today.

- Start each day by making progress against an A1.

- After you have opened and sorted your mail, handle each piece of paper only once – in other words only pick up a piece of paper from your in-tray when you intend to do something with it.

- Gather non-essential reading together and scan it for 20 minutes each week.

- Add additional actions to your personal action plan as they arise throughout the day and prioritise them.

- Each week complete the weekly jobsearch report (see next page) as an evaluation of how you are progressing against achieving your goals.

Procrastination is the thief of time. Do it now!

Don't be like a colleague of my friend Ann, who bought a motivational cassette tape on the subject of procrastination, but never got round to listening to it!

Job search performance and planning summary

Week ending (day/date):

THIS WEEK	GOALS FOR NEXT WEEK
I wrote _____ jobsearch letters	I will complete _____ applications
I sent ____ résumés and ____letters to potential employers	I will make _____ jobsearch telephone calls
I completed _____ applications	I will complete _____ hours of job research
I made _____ jobsearch telephone calls	I will set up _____ appointments for networking interviews
I completed _____ hours of job research	I will conduct ____ networking interviews
I set up _____ appointments for network interviews	I will follow up on _____contacts and _____ referrals
I conducted _____ networking interviews	
I received _____ invitations to a job interview	
I followed up on __ contacts and____ referrals	

Copyright waiver: This form may be photocopied for the personal use of the purchaser.

Personal daily action plan

Your name:		Date:	
Today's goals:			
Action plan:	A/B/C	Deadline	Completed

Uncompleted tasks to carry forward to tomorrow:

CHAPTER TWENTY

Networking: contact development

The benefits of networking and how to do it

'Putting off an easy thing makes it hard and putting off a hard one makes it impossible.'

George H. Lonmer

A new word has entered the English language in the past few years – 'networking' or contact development. For many people it's something they have been doing for years quite naturally. For others the thought of it makes them feel so uncomfortable that it makes the hairs on the back of their neck stand up.

Networking is the proactive process of maximising the relationships you already have and using these contacts to help you to identify work opportunities. Why is networking important? Some people believe that as few as 25 per cent of jobs are ever advertised. But someone must know about the rest! Also, career consultants will tell you that networking becomes increasingly important as you get older. About 50 per cent of people over the age of 40 find a job through personal contacts.

Networking is not about pestering people for a job to the point that none of your friends will ever speak to you. Neither is it about embarrassing people so that they feel morally obliged to help you, or even give you a job.

Networking is about approaching people genuinely to ask for advice and ideas on how you can get your next job – you aren't meeting them, telephoning or writing to them for a job. This is extremely important. When you make it quite clear that what you want from them is advice and ideas, you'll reduce their embarrassment about the contact and you will find them far more forthcoming.

On the practical front, just look at the power of numbers. Imagine you start off with the top 15 people in your network (see page 134), you contact these and they each give you the names of two of their contacts. That's an extra 30 people and you now have a network of 45. You speak to each of the new contacts and get two more names. You now have a network of 105 people and you contact your 60 new contacts and get two more names, now you're up to 225 . . . hang on, let's not get silly! There will be people you can't contact for whatever reason. I simply want to show that, using this process, it's not difficult to have 40 or 50 (or more!) people helping you in your jobsearch. People like to have their ego boosted by being asked for advice and I believe that most people will help if they are asked. You'll only embarrass them if it appears that you're asking them for a job.

Anyway, enough of their embarrassment! Broadcasting that you're on the dole (if you are) is a real ego booster for you isn't it? I think not! So how are you going to say it? Some people find it very difficult to tell others that they are looking for work, so if this barrier can be overcome quickly you will be able to start networking straight away. Look at the following expressions.

- **Words used to describe what has happened to an organisation**

Restructured	Gone bankrupt	We merged with another company
Contracted	Called in the receivers	We re-engineered
Downsized	The banks foreclosed	We had a change of management
Reorganised	We were taken over	We had a demerger

- **Words used to describe the effects it has on people**

Fired	Organised out	Dismissed	Booted out
Sacked	Let go	Axed	Dropped
Given P45	Said goodbye	Bounced	Let out
Made redundant	Surplus	Discharged	Terminated

In the space overleaf write down why you are looking for work. Don't be self-effacing and don't be critical of your (previous) employer.

Now say it four or five times out loud.

The 'bottom line' is still the same, but you should now feel a lot more comfortable in explaining to people why you're looking for work and why you're asking for their help and advice.

Who should I contact?

Many people think they have only a small network of personal contacts until they do this exercise. Go through your address book, diary, business card file, customer records, correspondence files, etc. and brainstorm. Write down the names of people you know in the appropriate spaces on the next two pages.

Once completed, these two pages will be some of the most valuable pages in this book. At this point include anyone and everyone you can think of. Ask your partner and close friends for ideas. You have started networking!

My network

Bankers	Competitors
Customers	Club members
Consultants	Doctors/dentist/solicitor

Friends	
Neighbours	Professional contacts
Suppliers	University/college/school colleagues
Past employers	Relatives
Teachers	Work colleagues

You can also develop 'virtual' contacts through Internet chat rooms and forums (see Chapter 29).

Now I've got my network, what next?

You need to identify who you should contact first from your network. They will be

- people you can contact relatively easily
- people high in the organisation – the higher the better
- people who could potentially employ you (even better)
- people on the same level as you, but with a different function, who can 'pass you on' to a peer.

  (People on the same level as you with the same function may see you as a competitor. People on a lower level are rarely useful except for information gathering.)

Now choose the top 15 names on your list and contact them. Decide which approach will be best. As a general principle, the first choice is to see them in person, second to telephone, third is write a letter and the least favoured option is to send an e-mail. Remember, your objective is not simply to inform people of the fact that you are looking for work, you want to motivate them to do something to help you. The more personal your contact, the more likely it is to succeed. Of course there are exceptions. If you're working in the Netherlands and have a friend in Japan who may be able to help you to get a job in California then e-mail might work. But then again it might not! Don't get me wrong. I'm not a technophobe and I couldn't do my job as a consultant and author without e-mail. It's excellent for maintaining business contacts and exchanging information, but as a starting point for network development it's my least favourite option.

Whatever you do, get to the point quickly and don't waste their time. Achieve your three objectives:

- **let them know you are looking for work** – so that they can keep their eyes and ears open
- **ask them for the names of two of their contacts** who you might approach
- **ask for their advice** about opportunities/recruitment consultants/ journals/ ads they might have seen.

Remember, you get one opportunity to make a first impression. The most powerful 'in' you can get is a personal introduction. As people give you names from their network do what you can to make a positive first impression.

Don't overstretch yourself by using the blunderbuss technique. If you try to contact everyone in your network on day one you won't be able to handle the workload. Keep prioritising and manage the project, for example follow up with a phone call if you've said you will.

Whenever you have made contact with one of your network, either in person or by telephone, send a short thank-you letter, or an e-mail! It costs little and shows your genuine appreciation.

Building a network doesn't happen in a day. Here are some great ideas for places and opportunities for building your network. They were kindly provided by Isobel Davies, an associate consultant and career coach with Macmillan International – and a member of my network!

Opportunities for network building (1)

Networking opportunities	Actions
Mentor someone	
Ask someone to mentor you	
Get involved in task forces or other exercises	
Send reports of your work to others who may be interested	
Talk to others about what they are doing in areas which may be of interest	
Look for development assignments or projects	

Networking opportunities	Actions
Plan regular reviews to talk about your performance and your development with your boss	
Prepare for your appraisal properly	
Keep a personal record of your projects and accomplishments	
Do a regular report on your and your team's exercises and send it to the people who might want to know	
When you dig out useful information, think about who else it might be interesting to, and forward it on	
Offer to present at other people's meetings and bring others in to talk at yours	
Attend training courses internally and externally	

Opportunities for network building (2)

Networking opportunities	Actions
Attend conferences and seminars	
Present at external events	
Write papers and articles about your work for external publishing	
Make time for the occasional supplier	
Subscribe to networks that can contribute knowledge and information about relevant topics	
Call one person a day that you would like to talk to, but isn't on your priority list	
Allow one evening a month for a drink after work with a friend or colleague that you don't see enough of	
And some of your own:	

Happy networking!

CHAPTER TWENTY-ONE

Using the telephone

Techniques to help you

'Speak clearly, if you speak at all; carve every word before you let it fall.'

Oliver Wendell Holmes

Used effectively, the telephone can get you past security guards, along hallowed corridors and into the offices of decision-makers!

Whether you are telephoning to confirm an appointment for an interview or at the start of your jobsearch, you will find the following tips, which are given to telesales people, helpful.

- Make sure you have a pen and paper ready, along with any relevant documents.

- Smile – I know it feels silly when you're the only one in the room, but it adds sparkle to your voice.

- Stand up! All your internal viscera are pushing up against your diaphragm and squeezing the confidence out of your voice. Standing up makes you more assertive and makes you sound more convincing!

- Have a clear objective of what you want to achieve, along with a fallback. For example, your primary objective may be to arrange an informal meeting; your secondary objective to call back tomorrow, when they have had a chance to read your resumé, to arrange a meeting.

- Make sure your language is convincing, fluent and understandable.

- Prepare your script in advance – write down your agenda.

- Practise your script – for example the direct approach: *'Hello Mr/Ms——— I'm———. You recently received a copy of my resumé. I'm calling to see if we can make an appointment to meet informally to discuss any vacancies you might have for management accountants.'*

- Have your diary ready!
- Keep a written record of every conversation.

Overcoming defences

The higher up the organisation you go, the higher and wider the barriers seem to become with receptionists and secretaries seemingly having no other purpose than to protect their bosses!

The higher up the organisation you go . . .

The following techniques range from the polite to the devious. All of them work!

- Find out the secretary's name from the receptionist. Address him/her personally and repeat the name at least twice when requesting to be put through.
- When you're networking and you're put through to a secretary, say it's 'a personal call' (most managers will take 'personal calls' since most of them think it's a call from a headhunter!). Get to the point quickly. If it's a friend of a friend, make sure you clarify it straight away.

- Beat the system by calling the manager at around 8.00 am or after 6.00 pm (i.e. before or after work for most secretaries) or when the secretary is at lunch.

- If you try phoning most companies during normal working hours and asking for the name of the marketing director, almost invariably the receptionist will tell you politely, but firmly, that they are not allowed to give that information over the telephone.

- Ring at around 8.30 pm and you're likely to speak to a lonely security guard, who is looking after the telephones along with the odd million pounds worth of building! Speak to them politely and explain that you want to call the marketing director the next day and you just wanted to make sure you'd got the right office. They'll be glad of someone to talk to and will probably reel off a list of names and extension numbers – if you ask for them, have your pen ready.

- Use a 'third-party recommendation' like 'Mr Robinson, your personnel manager has asked me to get in touch with . . .'

Remember, you may need to kiss a lot of frogs before you can find a prince! But persistence does pay!

CHAPTER TWENTY-TWO

Letters and e-mails

Tips and model formats

'A law of nature rules that energy cannot be destroyed. You change
its form from coal to steam, from steam to power in the turbine,
but you do not destroy energy. In the same way, another law
governs human activity and rules that honest effort cannot be lost,
but that some day the proper benefits will be forthcoming.'

Paul Speicher

If you can see someone in person, do it. If you can't see them personally, speak to them on the telephone. If you can't speak to them on the telephone, write a letter. If they are on the other side of the world or you can only get their e-mail address or you need a quick reply, send an e-mail. Both traditional 'snail-mail' and e-mail have their uses and, realistically, you will have to write a lot of letters and send a lot of e-mails. Learn from the people in direct marketing who write letters to customers for a living. Why? Because through your letters you are trying to sell another person the idea that 'they should meet you', that 'they should look at your CV', etc. When it comes down to it, it's a sales letter.

AIDA is the copywriter's best friend. If you look at well-written 'direct mail' letters they follow the AIDA format:

A   **Attention** – the first paragraph quickly comes to the point to grab the reader's attention.

I   **Interest** – the second gives information to arouse the reader's interest.

D   **Desire** – the third paragraph describes the benefits you will gain and what it will be like for you to own the product or service.

A   **Action** – now that you want the product or service, what do you do? Telephone, fill in a form, etc.

Sounds simple doesn't it? Would that it were that straightforward!

As you write letters of application, letters to networking contacts, letters to request application forms, covering letters to go with your CV, letters to recruitment consultants and e-mails, make sure that you check to see if they follow the AIDA principles.

Try to see the letter or e-mail from the recipient's viewpoint. What impression would it make on you? What would you do if you received it?

The following pages contain some general tips on letter writing which many people, who are unused to letter writing, find useful. After the 'model letters' there are some tips on using e-mail.

Letter writing tips

- Use good quality A4 paper; ideally 90 or 100 gsm. Matching envelopes create a good impression too. If you really want to push the boat out, get some stationery printed at your high street printshop. (Don't ask for the address to be printed in blue – it doesn't photocopy too well.)

- Handwriting is OK if it's legible. A word-processed letter is almost always OK, unless you have been specifically asked to submit a handwritten application. If you're using an inkjet printer, make sure it's set to the best print quality.

- There should be no spelling mistakes, grammatical errors or scruffy layout. But that can't happen! Don't you believe it! When I recruited a secretary recently I rejected over half of the applications for these reasons. The advertisement asked for 'accuracy'! Fortunately, modern software packages check as you type. If it's an older package make sure you run the spell-check and the grammar check.

- Write to a named person whenever you can.

- 'Dear Mr' is straightforward for men. If you don't know whether a woman is a 'Mrs' or 'Miss' then 'Ms' is the safest bet these days. These named letters end 'Yours sincerely' (small 's').

- When you have to write 'Dear Sir' or 'Dear Madam' (note, no 'e' at the end) then these letters end 'Yours faithfully' (small 'f').

- If an advertisement asks you to apply to Peter Butler do not start the letter 'Dear Peter' – it's over-familiar unless you know Peter personally. Even then be cautious, since your letter may be photocopied and circulated to other people.

- Be succinct – get to the point quickly. If your letter is more than one page long, then edit it to fit on one page.

- Match the skills and knowledge that you have to those the recruiter is looking for, i.e. those mentioned either in the job description or the advertisement.

- Never, never, never be self-effacing – 'I'm not quite what you're looking for but I'll give it a go anyway!' And don't point out anything that is missing from your portfolio of skills and knowledge. It's their job to spot that!

On the following pages I have included some sample letters. They are not offered as definitive examples but, hopefully, they will provide the spark of inspiration you need if you are sitting staring out of the window with a blank sheet of paper in front of you!

Warning! One of the wonderful things about modern word-processing packages is that you can do mail merges, cut and paste information, and copy files all with the click of a mouse and a few keystrokes. Check that the name at the start of the address matches the salutation (the Dear Mr or Ms bit). If you haven't got an eye for detail ask someone who has to proofread and check for you. Letters addressed to Colonel Mustard that start 'Dear Professor Plum' go straight into the bin! And take my word for it, it does happen.

Letter to request an application form

4 Stable Cottages
Abthorpe
Northamptonshire
NN12 8QT
Tel 123 7777777

23 March 2005

Mr G. Choice
Moderate Corporation
Science Park
Daventry Road
Northants
NN99 99NN

Dear Mr Choice

RE: CE/23393

I noticed your advertisement in the *Chronicle & Echo* newspaper for a laboratory supervisor. I would be very grateful if you will send me an application form.

I look forward to hearing from you.

Yours sincerely

Janet Dickson (Mrs)

Note

- Don't enclose a CV or anything else at this point. Follow their system.

Covering letter with CV

4 Stable Cottages
Abthorpe
Northamptonshire
NN12 8QT
Tel 123 7777777

23 March 2005

Mr G. Choice
Moderate Corporation
Science Park
Daventry Road
Northants
NN99 99NN

Dear Mr Choice

I would like to apply for the post of accounts supervisor which was advertised recently in the *Chronicle & Echo.*

I have read the job description with great interest and enclose my completed application form.

I look forward to hearing from you.

Yours sincerely

Janet Dickson (Mrs)

Notes

- Don't antagonise them by implying that you're bound to get an interview. If you are too presumptuous you'll turn them off.
- This letter does very little, however, to help the recruiter to match the candidate to the job. It would have been a good idea to include three or four feature, advantage or benefit statements (see Chapter 25).

Response to an advertised vacancy

4 Stable Cottages
Abthorpe
Northamptonshire
NN12 8QT
Tel 123 7777777

23 March 2005

Mr G Choice
Moderate Corporation
Science Park
Daventry Road
Northants
NN99 99NN

Dear Mr Choice

Ref: MCC/737 – Production manager: *Chronicle & Echo*, 22nd May 2005

I am writing in response to the above advertisement and wish to apply for
the position.

You will see from my CV that, for the past five years, I have managed a plant
manufacturing shampoos and hair colourants on a continuous production
basis. Many of the production features appear to be very similar to your
own. Previously I worked as Materials Planning Manager in a high-volume
batch production plant.

I believe I have all the qualities you have outlined in your advertisement; I
am ISO 9000 trained, a strong leader and have a capacity for hard work.

I am now seeking a position where my experience and expertise can be fully
utilised.

I look forward to hearing from you.

Yours sincerely

Janet Dickson (Mrs)

Note

● This letter highlights what the candidate has to offer against the
recruiter's requirements, but isn't a 'rewrite' of the CV.

A speculative letter to a targeted potential employer

4 Stable Cottages
Abthorpe
Northamptonshire
NN12 8QT
Tel 123 7777777

23 March 2005

Mr G. Choice
Moderate Corporation
Science Park
Daventry Road
Northants
NN99 99NN

Dear Mr Choice

Ref: An Opportunity to Increase Your Market Share and Reduce Operating Costs

As the Marketing Director (Electronic Products) of a £50m turnover UK company, I have initiated and managed improvement programmes that have reversed sales and profit declines.

Some of my achievements include:
- launching six new products over the last two years and increasing market share substantially
- increasing sales by 12% by exploiting new markets
- reducing marketing operation overheads by £125,000 by introducing effective controls
- introducing networked computer-based information and financial control systems to improve customer response times and invoicing
- sales and profit forecasting on a monthly basis with 90%+ accuracy.

My CV is enclosed as I am now actively looking for a new position. I would be very glad to give you more information or to come and see you.

Yours sincerely

Janet Dickson (Mrs)

Note

- Four or five achievement statements should be just right. You want to stimulate their interest and leave them wanting to know more.

Making something out of nothing

4 Stable Cottages
Abthorpe
Northamptonshire
NN12 8QT
Tel 123 7777777

23 March 2005

Mr G. Choice
Moderate Corporation
Science Park
Daventry Road
Northants
NN99 99NN

Dear Mr Choice

It was kind of you to read my CV and write to me on 19th March.

I was disappointed to learn that there are no openings in your company. It would have been a fortunate coincidence if my letter had reached you when you were recruiting for someone with my background.

May I ask you whether you can suggest the names of any other people whom I might contact?

I know that managers like yourself are often asked by others to 'keep their eyes open' for people with my skills and knowledge. I would very much appreciate you referring me to any of your acquaintances who might be interested. I will welcome any additional suggestions that you can give.

Many thanks in anticipation.

Yours sincerely

Janet Dickson (Mrs)

Note

- What have you got to lose? This letter is also worth trying with recruitment consultants – they may refer you to a 'competitor'.

Speculative letter to a recruitment consultant

4 Stable Cottages
Abthorpe
Northamptonshire
NN12 8QT
Tel 123 7777777

23 March 2005

Ms H Hunter
Choose Well Consultants
Northampton Road
Wappenham
Northants
NN99 9NN

Dear Ms Hunter

I am seeking a new appointment where my general management experience in the hotel and catering industry can be used. Any dynamic and developing business area which involves direct customer contact would particularly interest me. I am also keen to continue to develop my general management skills.

My present company is undergoing a period of substantial change and so I believe this an ideal opportunity to review my career to date and investigate other possibilities.

I am willing to relocate within Europe. My current remuneration package includes a basic salary of £36,000 per annum, a 10% (variable) bonus, fully expensed car, private healthcare and a non-contributory pension scheme.

I enclose my CV and would be glad of any advice you can provide.

Yours sincerely

Janet Dickson (Mrs)

Note

- Note that salary package details are included in approaches to recruitment consultants so that they can match you against vacancies. Also, different consultants often deal with jobs at different levels.

Follow-up thank-you letter after networking

4 Stable Cottages
Abthorpe
Northamptonshire
NN12 8QT
Tel 123 7777777

23 March 2005

Mr G. Choice
Moderate Corporation
Science Park
Daventry Road
Northants
NN99 99NN

Dear Mr Choice

Many thanks for meeting me last week. I really did appreciate the comments you made about the way I have embarked on my jobsearch.

Thank you also for putting me in contact with Simon and Pat. I have arranged to meet Pat next week, but Simon seems to spend all of his time in meetings – I'll keep trying!

I'll let you know how I get on.

Kind regards

Yours sincerely

Janet Dickinson

Notes

- This letter is far less formal than any of the others, but is still businesslike.

- If you promise a friend that you'll let them know how you got on, then do it – they want to know and in a couple of weeks they may have some new information for you!

E-mail tips

I'm sitting in my office in rural Lincolnshire and have been catching up on some of my mail. I have just dropped notes on the desks of a client in San Francisco, a friend in Los Angeles, a friend who lives three miles away and sent a proposal to a client in London. The whole job took less time than it takes to go to the post box! The wonders of e-mail. I think I heard some-where that it travels at 3,000 miles per second!

The use of e-mail has revolutionised the way many people work, and it varies from being the bane of people's lives to their most important work-ing tool. I spoke to a number of recruiters when researching this section and was told that about 60–70 per cent of applications now arrive by e-mail and it's rising.

The speed of information exchange can be phenomenal. You can see a job advertised in the morning's newspaper, e-mail for information and have submitted your e-mail application, with completed application form and attached CV, before you have had your second cup of coffee of the day! I heard a story of a London-based firm posting a secretarial vacancy on one of the large recruitment websites, at midday. By 2.00 pm they'd interviewed and appointed someone to start the next day. Clearly it doesn't always happen so quickly but there's a lesson there for us all!

Correct use of e-mail can augment the effectiveness of your jobsearch, so here are a few dos and dont's.

Do:

- Understand the difference between urgent and important. It's important that you contact people in the right way. But don't pressurise yourself into rushing and making mistakes just because you're communicating electronically.
- Keep your message short. I prefer to use a very short e-mail message along, with a 'proper' letter and a CV as separate attachments. Others prefer the letter of application in the body of the e-mail.
- Put your telephone number and address at the end of your e-mail.

- Print-off any attachments before sending to ensure that they are correctly formatted, especially if you have adjusted the margin settings on attachments.

- Check that the recipient can read your files if you are sending letter or CV attachments. It would appear that MS Word has become the 'standard' and I haven't yet had an occasion when someone couldn't read my MS Word files. But if you're using an unusual word processor, it's worth sending a quick message to say that you would like to apply for the job and attach a CV, and ask what format should be used for attachments. In a similar way, some companies block e-mails from free service providers, such as Hotmail, as a way of cutting down junk mail – so check.

- When writing e-mails you should adopt the same principles as when writing traditional letters. Ask yourself, 'What do you want the recipient to know and do when they have read your message?'

- Use an attention-grabbing subject line.

- Use short sentences (35 words at most).

- Use your spell checker and grammar checker.

- And even when you have used your spelling and grammar checkers, print the document, re-read it out loud to yourself and then ask someone else to proofread and check your application. Julia Cardis, the author of *The Complete Idiot's Guide to Finding Your Dream Job Online* uses the expression 'proofread until your eyes bleed'! Perhaps a little OTT and graphic, but it makes the point. So why all this fuss? Well typos, spelling mistakes, sloppy grammar and poor presentation feature all too frequently in job applications. And what does the recruiter do? Delete and goodbye!

Don't:

- 'Blast-mail'. I know it's easier and quicker to write one message and then group-send it to 20 or 30 recruiters, but put yourself in a recruiter's shoes. Which approach do you prefer, a personal approach or the blunderbuss?

- Use heavy shading or fancy formatting, or complicated graphics and photographs. Your message won't photocopy well and some companies use special filters to block large files and pictures, so that their information highways don't become congested.

- Send password-protected documents as attachments. Yes, it does happen. Your password protects your CV on your PC at work, so that colleagues can't read it. Then you see a job in the newspaper . . . Put yourself in the recruiter's shoes – you have had 60 applications for the same job. Are you really going to take the trouble to contact your mysterious candidate? Copy the information and paste into a new file, print to check that it retains its formatting. Send the new file as an attachment and then delete!

- Use smileys and emoticons.

- Delete your message once you have sent it. You'll want to refer to it if you get an interview.

- Be over-familiar. Remember this is a business contact, not a bit of banter with an old school mate.

- Keep resending messages in a two-way conversation. Delete all but the most recent message.

Speculative applications and approaches by e-mail

The same rules apply here as approaching someone using a conventional letter – remember the AIDA formula.

There are many ways to find out someone's e-mail address, such as telephoning a receptionist or sending a message to their company's postmaster, for example postmaster@Get-That-Job.co.uk. Most company websites contain e-mail addresses, but these are often only general enquiries addresses. If you want to target your approach you may have to do some digging. There are a number of Internet directory sites, such as *www.whowhere.com* and many search engines such as Google, Yahoo! and Netscape which provide access to e-mail directories. Not surprisingly the majority of sites cater for the USA, but the UK is catching up. One thing to bear in mind is that you might just find someone's personal or family e-mail address, and you might do more harm than good by sending an e-mail to them at home rather than work. Also, you'll need to be sure that you're sending your e-mail to the right Jane Doe!

CHAPTER TWENTY-THREE

Writing your CV

What to include, how to lay out yours

'When I see a bird that walks like a duck and swims like a duck, I call that bird a duck.'

Richard Cardinal Cushing

Imagine yourself in your smartest clothes, looking as well-groomed as you have ever looked in your life and carrying that facial expression of quiet (but not arrogant) confidence.

Your CV (curriculum vitae), or resumé, or as some call it 'personal and career history', is a written equivalent of the mental picture you have just formed.

In almost all the contacts you make, whether networking, speculative applications or responses to advertisements, your CV and introductory letter will make the difference as to whether or not you get an interview.

The decision between a 'regret' (sorry you've missed your chance), a 'regret, but hold' (you're not exactly what we're looking for at present but we'll keep your details on file) and an 'invite for interview' can be made in as little as 30 seconds! I am being serious – that immaculately presented CV, beautifully written letter of application and the application form that took you two hours to write can be scanned by a recruiter and a decision made in less than a minute!

If you think this is unrealistic then look at it from the recruiter's side and pity Geoff, a colleague of mine, who advertised two jobs in a car assembly plant and got 1,400 replies! If Geoff had spent just one minute looking at each application that would have taken 1,400 minutes or a total of almost 24 hours non-stop! Beth, another friend, who is a personnel manager, was so overwhelmed with responses to an advertisement for a secretary that all applications in brown envelopes and all applications with second-class stamps were rejected. Two hundred responses to an advertisement is not at all uncommon. With applications online it can be even more, and you may find yourself competing with people from all parts of the globe. You see recruitment is a (legal) positive discriminatory process! The recruiter is 'filtering out' all those people who don't match the selection criteria, and keeping those who do. When you apply to larger organisations, or through a recruitment agency or through a website, you may well find that your application is even scanned by software for word-matches – these are called 'keywords'. If the software doesn't find the criteria the recruiter is looking for the software generates an automatic 'thank-you but no thank-you' e-mail . . . and maybe all because you typed ProductManager instead of Product Manager.

You need to help the recruiter positively to 'screen you in'. The job of your CV is to take you through the screening process to an interview. We'll look at online applications in Chapter 29.

Recruiters are all different

There is an expression that goes 'If you are ill and ask three Harley Street specialists for a second opinion then you'll get five different opinions'! In the same way recruiters have personal preferences in how they like to see CVs written. For this reason I can't offer dogmatic advice and say this is the way you MUST present your CV. Added to which, your CV is a very personal document – in the final analysis you are the best judge of whether your CV best represents you.

On page 164 is a 'CV summary' which will help you to gather the relevant information and some sample CVs to help you to decide on which layout you like best can be found on pages 168–177.

Basic principles

- Use clean laser-printed originals with a legible font, and stick to one font. The fonts without the bobbly bits like Arial and Helvetica, shown below, are called sans-serif (sans = French for without), the serifs on fonts like Times New Roman are there to help your eye to move quickly as you read. If your CV is a long document, with lots of information, you might choose to use a font with serifs. If it's short and you want the reader to savour every word use a sans-serif font.

This is in 8 point Times New Roman PS

`This is in 10 point New Courier`

This is in 12 point Helvetica

- Use good quality paper of 90 or 100 gsm. Either use a quality high white or a softer Old English white. Avoid pretty pastel shades!

- Be brief – use one or two pages if possible. You can do it! Screening of CVs is brief. If the most relevant item is on page 7 paragraph 6, forget it! And PLEASE, PLEASE don't use more pages than you need to! One or two, or maybe three if you must, but don't go on to twenty-eight pages, as I saw with one candidate. Honestly!

- Beware of jargon! – write in plain English if you are a logistics manager, a military officer, a research scientist, etc. Indeed, if you are a specialist of any kind, you will almost certainly have your own vocabulary. Use plain English!

- Be specific – 'I have five years' experience in . . .' says far more than 'I have wide experience of . . .', as does 'I reduced inventory from £4.2m to £1.8m in a period of 12 months' compared with 'We made substantial savings by reducing our inventory'.

- Even if you can produce a decent letter it may be worth investing in getting someone to do your CV for you. If you need help with the content then you may need a professional CV writer. On the other hand a professionally trained secretary can do wonders in terms of improving the presentation. Local newspapers and newsagents' windows are a good source. Ask to see previous examples and make sure they give you a copy of the file for future updating, and so that you can 'personalise' key strengths to produce a targeted CV to fit each job. Some of the modern software packages have CV templates, but before you decide to use a template, make sure that you're comfortable with the style, layout and content. It's your CV. And remember, if you're using the CV builder that came with your word processor it may end up looking just the same as all the other applicants using the same software.

- Proofread, proofread, proofread. Start at the bottom of the page and read backwards. You may thimk there are no mistakes, but by reading backwards you see each word in isolation and can spot errors and misspellings. For example, did you spot 'thimk' in the last sentence or did you read what you thought was there?

- If you have a name which may be interpreted as male or female, such as Jay or Frankie, enter 'm' or 'f' in brackets. I'm certainly not advocating sexual discrimination in recruitment, but it puts recruiters off balance when they phone candidates and get their sex wrong! If you think your name might cause confusion, help recruiters by explaining. Name: Malcolm (given) Hornby (family). And if you were named Rebecca at birth and have since then been known only as Becky, then put Becky on your CV. Remember it's YOUR marketing tool.

- Some recruiters like a wide margin on the left-hand side so that they can make notes.

- CVs often get separated from letters of application. Use the header and footer facility to ensure that your name and address are on each page – it will help if pages do become separated. It will also help an interviewer to remember your name when they are halfway through an interview and they've turned over the page!

- Presentation 'gimmicks' – personally I like to receive CVs from people who have had them bound or who have included a photograph. It says that they are prepared to put that bit of extra effort into their application. I know, however, that many of my fellow human resources professionals would strongly disagree. Your decision has to be based on the job and what you know about the organisation.

- If you're applying for your first job or are returning to work after bringing up a family, help the recruiter to recognise your transferable skills. 'President of the outdoor pursuits society' and 'qualified mountain leader' implies leadership and someone trained to cope with adversity. 'Treasurer of the parish church council' implies financial skills and abilities to deal with contractors etc. Spell it out for them.

The language of CVs

'It ain't what you say, it's the way that you say it.' This is not totally true, but there is an element of truth to it! Striking a balance between being positive and sounding arrogant can be a real challenge.

Use active words and not passive words. 'I was responsible for managing a project team which installed a new intranet' says more than 'I was involved in installing a new intranet'. The first statement is far more powerful, while the second might mean no more than you plugged it in and switched it on!

Avoid passive words such as liaised with, coordinated and administered. Use some of the following action verbs when writing your CV and also for letters of application.

Action verbs

accelerated	extended	reduced	terminated
accomplished	finished	reorganised	traced
achieved	generated	revised	traded
approved	implemented	scheduled	trained
conceived	improved	serviced	transferred
conducted	increased	simplified	translated
completed	introduced	set up	trimmed
consolidated	launched	sold	tripled
created	maintained	solved	turned
decided	negotiated	started	uncovered
delivered	ordered	structured	united
demonstrated	performed	streamlined	utilised
designed	pioneered	strengthened	vacated
developed	planned	stressed	waged
directed	processed	stretched	widened
doubled	programmed	succeeded	won
eliminated	promoted	summarised	worked
ended	proposed	superseded	wrote
established	purchased	supervised	
expanded	redesigned		

But beware – don't overdo it. The recruiter is looking for a mortal!

Try reading the finished version of your CV to your partner or close friend. If you go a little pink you're probably spot on – bright red and you've over-done it!

How to avoid convoluted and imprecise expressions 'Brevity is best'

Avoid	Use
As a result of this project the company's costs were cut by . . .	This cut costs by . . .
During the period referred to in the previous sentence . . .	I . . .
As a consequence of the success of this project, I was asked to take up the more senior appointment of . . .	I was promoted . . .
In this position I . . .	I . . .
Considerable elements of my responsibilities were . . .	I was responsible for . . .
anticipate	expect
behind schedule	late
prior to	before
personnel	people
proceeded to	then
inaugurated	set up
initiated	started
terminated	ended

CV checklist

This checklist combines the should be (bold) and could be (italic) included items. Use this in combination with the CV summary on page 164 to help you to gather information and to develop your own CV.

- **Name, address, e-mail and telephone number(s) stating daytime contact.**
- *Marital status.*
- *Number of dependants and ages.*
- *Nationality.*
- *Date of birth/age.*
- **School, college/university attended – normally only from age of 11 onwards, unless you're a school leaver or recent graduate.**
- **Qualifications – for a school leaver or recent graduate looking for a first job state GCSEs and GCEs (level, subjects and pass grade) along with subjects taken and class of degree. For a 45 year old divisional director, 6 'O' levels, 3 'A' levels, BSc 2(i) Chemistry is usually sufficient, although for some professions, for example accountancy, you may wish to include GCE 'A' level grades.**
- *Language proficiency.*
- *Willingness to relocate – especially if you're out of commuting distance (omit if you aren't).*
- **Current/last job – state this first, then work backwards through your career, allocating most space to recent job(s) with brief mentions of your early career. Give a one- or two-sentence summary of the company products/services and their annual turnover, summarise your responsibilities and achievements against each job.**
- *Current/last salary and benefits package, for example company car. Be brief. Opinions differ on whether salary should be included – you may wish to keep your cards close to your chest and risk missing an opportunity because they think you'll be 'too expensive'.*
- *Career aims.*
- *Personal strengths.*

- *Leisure activities be realistic; a one-week skiing holiday five years ago does not qualify you as a skier! Include a variety to show that you have broad interests, but not too many – they may think you'll have no time left for work! Three to four interests should be adequate.*

- *Professional achievements – for example titles of research papers or articles you have had published. But don't, like someone who once sent me a 28-page CV, attach the papers!*

- *Memberships of professional institutions and whether by examination or election.*

- *Do not include names of referees, unless you are applying for a job in the public sector.*

- *Driving license – clean and current don't mean the same!*

You need to help the reader positively to 'screen you in'

CV summary

Name:	Address:	Tel. and e-mail:

Strengths – four or five short sentences about your personal strengths. A four- or five-sentence summary of your career; who you are and what you have to offer. Make every word count!

Education and qualifications – right here up front if you have a first class honours degree, PhD, MBA. You may wish to leave to the end if your business achievements outshine your academic ones!

Career history – most recent first and work backwards. Include responsibilities and quantified achievements. Reduce the information as you go back, for example give, five achievements for your current/most recent job, three from a job two years ago, but only one from a job 15 years ago.

Professional memberships etc.

Personal information – Willingness to relocate, interests, marital status, etc.

'Readymade' templates

Many of today's word-processing packages contain excellent pre-formatted CV templates, but beware of their limitations (see earlier in this chapter) There are also lots of ideas to be had from the jobsites on the Internet. Experiment with the different styles and formats until you find one that you're most comfortable with.

Leaving the forces – or any highly technical environment?

Mind your language when writing your CV! Now what does he mean by that? All professions have their own jargon and expressions. If you're an accountant looking for a job as an accountant, you can talk to an interviewer in accountantspeak, or a surgeon talking to another surgeon . . . and so on. If you are 'stepping out' into civvy street you'll need to use a different language to the one you're used to using.

To give you an example. I live in Lincolnshire and there are four RAF bases within 15 minutes drive. I even get my own private air show occasionally when the Red Arrows practise over my house! Recently, I was asked to give advice on the CV of a friend of a friend who is leaving the RAF. The first thing that struck me was his rank/job title of 'technician' – there was no further explanation. A chat over the phone revealed that he's a highly skilled, highly qualified engineer and is responsible (along with others) for making sure that about 40 million pounds' worth of aircraft works as it should. Years ago I used to be involved in recruiting semi-skilled 'manufacturing technicians', who were process workers on a shampoo production line. Have I made my point?

Prospective employers may have little or no knowledge of the specialist skills and attributes that you use in your service role, or the ways in which these can be transferred across to civilian jobs. As a result of this, they may be reluctant to take you on an as an unknown quantity.

When you write your CV and letters of application, and when you go to interviews, make sure that you explain what your current job involves along with your responsibilities, in plain English that can be understood by non-specialists. **Stress your transferable skills.** This is especially important if you have to send your CV to a personnel department or a recruitment agency. The people responsible for the initial screening are often non-specialists involved in recruiting people for many different kinds of jobs.

If you have served in the armed forces at any time in your life, the following may be able to help you in your jobsearch:

- Regular Forces Employment Association – tel 020 7321 2011 for your local branch, or *www.rfea.org.uk*
- Officers' Association – tel 020 7930 0125, or *www.officersassociation.com*
- SSAFA – tel 020 7403 8783 for your local branch or *www.ssafa.org.uk*

Examples of resumés/CVs

If you're sitting in front of a blank PC screen saying, 'where do I begin?' then I hope the following pages of sample CVs will help you to write your own.

None of the examples should be taken as definitive. Each is unique to the person who wrote it. They are CVs from real people and each of them has 'worked' because it helped the writer to *Get That Job!* I hope that you will be able to take learning points from each to enable you to develop your own unique, personal and effective CV. Use the table below to help summarise the most useful points. Remember, it's **YOUR CV**, it's not a confessional! It's a marketing tool.

(Please note that names and places of work on the CVs have been changed for confidentiality).

Learning points from other people's CVs	
Things I like – to be used in my CV	**Things I don't like – to be avoided in my CV**

Note: it is a good idea to print your CV single-sided – if only because it makes it easier to photocopy!

STEVEN JOHNSON
22 Coventry Road, Edgbaston
Birmingham B66 77BM
Home tel: (0303) 30303
e-mail: Steven@Johnson.oc.ku

Highly motivated, energetic 44 year old senior manager having successfully achieved objectives through developing people. A natural leader with strong interpersonal and communication skills, who thrives on being involved in leading teams in an environment of creativity and constant challenge. Responsible for results of a keenly focused team in terms of sales, quality and profitability. Displays initiative and a positive outlook to all challenges, ideas generator, decisive and highly adaptable to change. Extensive experience and knowledge of both general and sales management with an in-depth understanding of the people business.

ACHIEVEMENTS

Developed teams of managers monitoring both personal performance and that of the sales units, ensuring objectives achieved together with quality and service standards being maintained.

Created a competitive team spirit whereby individual and collective performance was recognised. Provided league tables, instigated competitions, produced interesting and varied communication formats.

Energised team, created environment ensuring national sales campaigns were tackled enthusiastically with success being achieved and measured in improving performance position. Appointed and managed new direct sales force including sales meetings, one-to-one coaching and field visits. Developed and nurtured relationships with sales units to achieve common business objectives, resulting in business levels being increased by 140% over a six-month period.

Produced quarterly/annual business plans to ensure focus and direction to achieving business and quality objectives.

Instigated and developed a programme and systems for achieving total quality management resulting in customer service complaints being reduced by 28% in three months.

Responsible for staff recruitment at junior management level. Disciplinary matters and general personnel responsibilities including managing staff budgets.

Responsible for quarterly/annual appraisal process whereby individuals recognise critical success factors which are incorporated within a personal development plan.

Involved with the training of staff both within units and at the area training centre. Follow-up process adopted to ensure training benefits maximised.

Took part in strategic projects from inception to final presentation enabling project management skills to be developed to the full.

Conducted regular meetings and one-to-one discussions using consultative planning approach agreeing action points to ensure progress.

STEVEN JOHNSON ctd

<u>CAREER PROGRESSION</u>   **1979–present**   **Stable Building Society**

2004–present	**Area Sales Manager**	Midlands
	Responsible for 16 Managers, 135 staff	
	Report to the Area Sales Director	
2003–2004	**Regional Sales Manager**	East Midlands
	Responsible for 8 Managers, 4 Direct Sales	
2002–2003	**Regional Manager**	Coventry
2001–2002	**Assistant Regional Manager**	Coventry
2000–2001	**Branch Manager**	Harrogate
1993–2000	**Branch Manager**	Crewe
1987–1993	**Branch Manager**	Maidenhead
1979–1987	**Junior Management/Senior Clerical**	Various locations

<u>PERSONAL DEVELOPMENT</u>

March 1997	Sundridge Park Management Centre
November 1993	Peters Management Consultants (Sales Training)
December 1981	Ashridge Management College
	Extensive Internal Training covering a wide range of topics.

<u>ADDITIONAL INFORMATION</u>
Married – 1 child (19)
Fellow Chartered Building Society Institute
School Governor/Chairman of charitable trust
Past member of Round Table, holding a number of offices including chairman
Computer literate – all Microsoft Office software packages

<u>INTERESTS</u>
Gardening, golf, badminton, stamp collecting, trying to keep fit.

PETER RADLETT
14 Greenview
Central Milton Keynes
MK98 89MK
Tel: (987) 676767 Mobile: 1000 6987654
e-mail: Peter@Radlett.oc.ku

CAREER PROFILE

Experienced and versatile manager with strong leadership skills. Knowledge of high technology applied to a variety of product-based organisations. Commercially aware. Adept at introducing change either in the organisation or by the introduction of capital investment, and who recognises that high productivity is only achieved through a knowledgeable and motivated team.

ACHIEVEMENTS

- Implemented a £4 million investment programme on a greenfield site through the installation and commissioning of four discrete product lines.
- Implemented capital investment programme to reduce reliance on external suppliers of key components.
- Introduced the concept of operator process control by use of a series of training modules.
- Recruited, trained and motivated the production team to develop and grow the business.
- Implemented new production planning routines to reduce generation of works documentation from 10 days to 4 days.
- Reduced inventory holding on major product lines from 15 weeks to 5 weeks.
- Developed, through training, line management supervision.
- Reduced losses by improved monitoring and feedback to suppliers.

CAREER HISTORY

2004–Present OPMKS Ltd, Milton Keynes – Manufacturing Manager, responsible to Operations Director, for all aspects of manufacture for photographic enlargers in a vertically integrated organisation

2003–2004 TISSUE Group, Hemel Hempstead – Production Manager, responsible to Operations Director, for all aspects of manufacture for Tissue Culture Products

2001–2003 VENTILATORS Ltd, High Wycombe – Production Manager, responsible to Manufacturing Director, for line production, line planning and stock control

1995–2001 HYDRAULIC MOTORS Ltd, High Wycombe – Manufacturing Manager, responsible to General Manager, for purchasing, production planning, stock control, production engineering, machining, assembly and despatch

PETER RADLETT ctd

EDUCATION AND QUALIFICATIONS

1984–1986	Hemel Hempstead Polytechnic – HND in Mechanical Engineering
1998	High Wycombe College of Further Education – Certificate in Computing Studies
1999	High Wycombe College of Further Education – Member, Institute of Industrial Managers (IIM)

MANAGEMENT TRAINING

1973	Guardian Business School – accountancy for non-financial managers
2003–2004	Paradigm Shifters – leadership and decision-making skills

INTERESTS

Squash, home improvements, computing, walking and classic cars.

ROBERT GREEN
Ivybridge House
Manchester road
Stalybridge
M99 99M
Tel: (669) 99991. Mobile: 1234 7654321. e-mail: Rob@Green.oc.ku

****

**An experienced manager with design, technical and sales skills. Have designed numerous products including bedroom/kitchen ranges and occasional furniture. prepared technical details of products including packaging. Handled numerous sales enquiries/contracts, liaising with clients at all levels. Assembled and fitted products including bedroom and kitchen ranges.

****

ACHIEVEMENTS

- Designed many successful products for mail order and high street clients including a new bedroom range by Bedroom Sellers and Housefitters.
- Handled door contracts with national companies from enquiries through to production.
- Designed and erected exhibition stands both in the UK and abroad.

EXPERIENCE

Bedrooms Ltd   2003–present
Manchester   **Development Manager**

Responsible for design and development of all the company's new products from conception through to production. This involved accurate preparation of production drawings using AutoCAD, material and fittings specifications, packing design and instruction leaflets. On the sales side I handled all the company's incoming door and component enquiries, liaising closely with customers on technical matters. I had a staff of five and was responsible for CNC programming and the development workshop.

Components Ltd   1987 – 2003
Lancashire   **Development Manager**

Commenced my career as design draughtsperson working my way to Development Manager on leaving. I was responsible for all aspects of design and development work including aesthetic, economic and production considerations. Was required to draw up and meet planning timetables; producing sketches and cost for short-listed designs. Was involved with presentation and selling of product, pricing and quotations. I produced detailed customer assembly leaflets and was responsible for a busy development workshop.

Shell Oil Refinery   1984–1987
Cheshire   **Process Operator**

Responsible for efficient running of petrol refinery plant.

Bolton Borough Council   1979 – 1984
Bolton   Clerk/Draughtsman
I gained experience in several different aspects of a council department, including
printing, preparation of artwork, and furniture design. I planned kitchen layouts for
home economics rooms in schools and colleges

EDUCATION AND TRAINING

Bolton Technical High School
GCE 'O' levels in English Language, Mathematics and Technical Drawing.

Manchester College of Furniture
Trained for design and construction of furniture.

FIRA
Various day courses and seminars

Bolton College of Further Education
City and Guilds in computer aided draughting and design using AutoCAD.

HOBBIES AND PASTIMES

I am a married man with two children. My interests include most sports but
particularly fishing. I live close to moorland and do a lot of walking. I maintain and
improve our house and do most of my own car maintenance.

CATHERINE SCARLET
14 Severn View, Bristol, BS99 9AA
Tel: 1234 56789 (home), 1234 98765 (mobile)
E-mail: Catherine@Scarlet.oc.ku

Finance director with general management, company development and acquisition experience combined with practical operating skills in the investment banking, broking, chemical processing and retail distribution industries. Special abilities include:

- Managing change, turning round underperforming activities.
- Forming, managing and motivating teams, developing individuals.
- Developing profitable relationships, negotiating business deals.
- Analysing, evaluating and managing company acquisitions.

CAREER

Lotsacash Investment Bank Group, 2001-present
Operations Director, Capital Markets & Treasury, 2001 – present
- Responsible for efficient operation of capital markets/treasury financial control, settlements and computer operations. 100 staff, budget £10m.
- I was headhunted to turn round ineffective accounting, computer and treasury control system.
- Rebuilt teams, improved staff quality and training, reduced staff and overtime without disruption, significantly improved management information and operating efficiency.
- Investigated and negotiated joint-venture arrangements in Europe.

Broking International plc, 1992–2001
Commercial Director, 2000–2001
- Responsible for the London-based broking businesses. T/O £75m, profit £9m, 500 staff.
- Conducted start-up of German bond-broking business.
Financial Director, Management and Securities Division, 1995–2000
- Responsible for advising the Board on worldwide financial and related management matters. T/O £113m, profit £22m, 90 staff.
- Close involvement with acquisitions in UK, USA, Germany, Luxembourg, Hong Kong, Singapore and Australia and with subsequent business development.
Group Financial Controller, 1992–1995
- Improved full range of management systems and controls in media advertising and broking exercises.
- Contributions in the job led to promotion to Financial Director.

Stackem High Stores, 1991–1992
Internal consultant, Retail Stores Division
- Investigated, recommended and implemented the integration of two stores groups.

CATHERINE SCARLET ctd

Springy Sofas Ltd, 1990
Managing Director
- Planned and brought new factory to full production of moulded urethane components.
- Developed market strategy and customer base of group. T/O £3m, profit £160k.

QUALIFICATIONS
BA Accountancy and Law 2/1, University of Bristol 1982
CA gained with Price Waterhouse, 1985

PERSONAL
Age 46 years. Married, two children. Health excellent. Interests – family, antiques, aerobics, Greek mythology (launched and maintain special interest, Internet community website: *www.GreekGeeks.co.uk*)

JANET WAITE
58 Desmond Road
London
NW19 9DE
Tel: (020) 055 5656, Mobile: 09876544567890. e-mail: JWAITE@ssd.moc

PROFILE
An effective personnel generalist with skills in team-building and gaining
commitment from senior management through persuasion.

Enjoys deadlines and performs well under pressure. Gives wholehearted
commitment to a task and displays a high degree of tenacity and resilience when
facing difficult situations.

Outside the work environment enjoys being stretched and, for example, has, in the
last few years, taken up skiing, windsurfing and paragliding.

CAREER
Very Wealthy Banks (Investments) plc   2000–present
Based in the City with 2,500 employees in a highly IT-oriented environment

Personnel Manager: 2005–present
Settlement Services Division
A strongly generalist role, responsible for the provision of an effective professional
service to c.900 staff. Managing a team of six personnel staff. My achievements in
this role have been:
- Following significant cutbacks, selected to contribute to re-structuring.
- Charged with the task of detailed project planning and execution for the transfer
  of personnel activities back to line managers.

Personnel Manager Information Technology   2002–2005
Managing a team of five staff (including three professional personnel officers)
covering strongly systems development oriented client areas, c.550 staff. My
achievements in this position were:
- Worked with the senior management team to revise job roles and restructure
  a)   the Systems Development and Support department resulting in the
       reduction of 30 staff and
  b)   the Management Services department resulting in the reduction of 50 jobs.
- Established a new personnel team of five from scratch – recruited, analysed
  training needs and coached for their improved job performance through regular
  meetings and improved communications. Heightened team contribution and
  helped them to develop in their own roles.
- Implemented psychometric testing to determine analytical skills, and
  assessment centre techniques to clarify project management potential, ensuring
  the cost effective application of training programmes.
- Successfully implemented the appraisal policy within client area, running
  courses and successfully working to overcome management resistance to
  objective setting.

Principal Personnel Officer: Business Development Department   2001–2002
- In a predominantly sales and marketing environment managed 3 staff, in a
  generalist role serving staff in the south east, UK regional offices and New York,
  but also with emphasis on recruitment and remuneration.

JANET WAITE ctd

- Gained acceptance to the establishment of career paths for Business Development department staff involving progress through customer support, UK sales, international sales and the New York office.
- Creative and analytical approach to recruitment into a number of key roles, according to a specification which required a unique combination of financial services, computer industry and sales/marketing expertise.

Senior Personnel Officer   2000–2001

A generalist role, covering the Systems Development and Sales and Marketing departments. Particularly involving recruitment and development (graduate and YTS); and experience in HAY-based job evaluation. Achievements in this position were:

- Sold new salary review concepts to line managers and worked with them in resolving the remuneration-level problems which were leading to high turnover of specialist staff.
- Initiated an in-house recruitment event to appeal to computer scientists, gained the commitment of the senior management to participate in the event and achieved recruitment targets.

Big Boat Builders, Research & Development   1998–2000

Research, development and production of electronic equipment, 2,500 staff

Senior Personnel Officer – Recruitment

Responsible for the recruitment of professional, technical, manual, clerical and secretarial staff. Involved in the recruitment of graduates and professional engineers. Achievements in the position were:

- Became the driving force behind the use of psychometric testing for the recruitment of specialist, high value staff. By means of presentations to senior management gained acceptance for this approach.
- Ran a series of 'walk-in interviews' to attract scarce technical skills and validated its cost effectiveness.

Car Parts Ltd   1994–1998

Manufacture and distribution of automotive parts, approx. 2,500 staff. Successive appointments in this heavily unionised environment. Trainee, Salaries and Records Administrator, Personnel Officer, Systems Coordinator, Recruitment and Salaries Adviser.

Electronic Switching Ltd   1992–1993

Import/Export Sales Coordinator.

EDUCATION AND TRAINING

Chartered Member of the Chartered Institute of Personnel and Development (2001)
BSc Combined Hons Degree in Science (Zoology/Geography)

Psychometric Testing

Registered user of ASE-nferNelson (all instruments), Kostic PAPI (Perception and Preference Inventory), Saville and Holdsworth (OPQ and Aptitude Tests)

PERSONAL

Age: 36. Single. Interests include: Windsurfing, skiing, hill walking, watching motor racing, keep Siamese cats and enjoy theatre.

CHAPTER TWENTY-FOUR

How to complete application forms

Why and how you should complete them

'The mode in which the inevitable comes to pass is through effort'

Oliver Wendell Holmes

What an imposition – you spend all that time writing your CV, spot an ad in the newspaper for a job that sounds perfect and you ring to ask for details. They send you an information pack and an application form. Why should you now waste time completing an application form?

It would be much easier to fill in your name and address at the top of the application form and write 'please see attached CV' – you might get away with it but you probably won't!

Organisations use application forms for two main reasons.

- To collect 'standard information' on all candidates, so that the person doing the initial screening can easily compare candidates against each other and against the job.

- So that candidates are 'forced' to provide important information. For example, a CV may simply state 'full driving licence' whereas the response to the application question 'Give details of any driving licence endorsements' may reveal '9 penalty points; 3 × speeding'.

Looked at from one viewpoint, an application form is a chore; from a positive viewpoint, it is your perfectly targeted CV!

Completing application forms

- Read the form through before writing anything.

- Take a photocopy of the blank form and use it to draft your answers.

- Complete the form as requested. Black ink and block capitals doesn't mean blue ink (no matter how dark) and hieroglyphics!

- If you need to expand any of the sections onto extra pages, write your name and the job applied for at the top of each page.

- Match your application to the job – review the job advertisement and any information you have received and match your application to the job.

- Answer all the questions.

- Explain any gaps in your career.

- Maximise the 'Other information' opportunity by making a positive 'you' statement – see Chapter 31.

- Use feature and benefit statements to relate your past experience to the skills and qualities they are looking for – see Chapter 25. Don't include *any* negatives about yourself – this is not the place to be self-effacing.

- Telephone referees before putting them on the application. First, as a courtesy but second, to help them to help you by bringing out your best points when they give a reference. You want them to emphasise your particular skills which are most relevant to the job.

- Proofread, proofread, proofread – and get someone else to do it.

- Photocopy the completed form – so that you know what you've said when you are invited for interview, and to add to your brag box!

- Use first-class postage or, if the organisation is local, make an opportunity to 'be in the area' and deliver it by hand (in the same clothes that you would wear for an interview). You never know, you might even get a chance to meet the recruiter, or at least his or her secretary – an opportunity to make a positive impression, distinguish yourself from the competition and increase the memorability of your application! And if the application form is bulky, then double check that there's enough postage on the envelope. I recently heard a sad story of a very senior local government official who was 'invited' to apply for a position. (In other words the job's yours but we've got to go through the formalities of advertising and interviewing!) The candidate spent a weekend completing the lengthy application form, posted it off in plenty of time and waited to hear. The deadline came and went and, as the interview date got nearer, he waited for his interview invitation. It didn't arrive. He rang and was told they had never received his application. A couple of days later, the applicant received the application pack which he had posted, endorsed 'Return to sender – DNA' (delivery not accepted). The clerk in the post room had refused to accept the package because there was a postage surcharge. The moral is obvious – check! If you want to be doubly sure and impress, use Special Delivery or Datapost. Or for a top job why not use a courier service like UPS or DHL?

Online applications

(See also Chapter 29 'Finding your job on the Net')

Take your time and be as thorough as you would if you were writing by hand. Print off the questions and compose your replies in your word processor – so that you can copy them into the form. Many applications have a word count limit for different sections to force the applicant to be concise. Use the word count facility to keep checking and be ruthless – it's amazing what you can edit out of documents and still retain the meaning.

Recruiters will hate me for suggesting this, but why not try a few jobs that you wouldn't dream of really applying for as practice, before you start applying for real? It doesn't cost anything and all you'll lose is the time it took you to complete the form! Also remember that when you do 'go live', the process will take a number of stages, and will also require you to check a number of times and then to confirm before you click 'submit'.

Read the advertisement and try to second-guess any special requirements or words that they'll be looking for. There's a very good chance that your application will be scanned by dedicated software, programmed to look for keywords and reject your application if they aren't there.

When you're completely satisfied that you have got it right, and have checked your spellings for the last time, go back online and copy and paste your text into their application form.

Do a final check and click 'submit application'. You'll probably get an e-mail acknowledgement almost instantly. Don't get too excited – the software's programmed to do that as well. Good luck!

CHAPTER TWENTY-FIVE

Selling yourself

Your features and benefits

'What we hope ever to do with ease, we must learn first to do with diligence'

Samuel Johnson

What has selling got to do with getting a job? – I'm a teacher, nurse, accountant, van driver, . . . Well, whatever job you want, while you are actively job hunting you are constantly selling yourself whether by letter, telephone, e-mail or interview.

Contrary to what you might think 'selling' isn't only about charm, a smile and a pleasant personality. These are part of it but the selling process goes far beyond.

Most experts would agree that the basic core of any selling process involves the following.

Beforehand:

Objective setting	Identifying what you hope to get out of the contact.

During:

Presenting opening benefits	Getting quickly to the point so that the other person can see what's in it for them.
Probing for needs	Using 'how, why, what, when, where and who' questions to help you understand requirements.
Presenting benefits	Helping the other person to see the relevance of what you have to offer.
Overcoming objections	Outweighing any reservations they might have with the benefits you can offer.
Closing	Ending the contact with an agreement of a positive outcome.

Presenting benefits

The process of presenting benefits is one which many people find difficult, so let's have a look at what's involved.

Features → Advantages → Benefits

People buy products or services not for what they are, but for what they can do for them. In the same way, companies recruit employees not for who or what they are, but for what they bring to the company and what they can do for it.

What's the benefit of benefits?

I bought a mower with a 42-inch cutter deck because it meant that I wouldn't have to waste too much time cutting the grass. BENEFIT – I can do other things that I enjoy doing!

I bought an answerphone with a remote interrogation facility, so that when I stay away from home I can still keep in touch with my business contacts. BENEFIT – I keep in touch and don't miss out on business opportunities.

Benefit statements turn your gobbledygook into language which the other person can understand and is relevant to them.

By using benefit statements you will help the recruiter to understand any technical jargon you may be using and help them see the relevance of what you've done before the job you're being interviewed for.

Remember, in recruitment the recruiter is a 'customer' who is deciding whether to 'buy' your service for their company.

Feature	Advantage	Benefit
A description of product or service	Says what the feature does	Answers 'what's in it for me?'
A fact or characteristic	Says what the feature means	Answers what the features and advantages will ultimately mean to the user
A property or attribute of a product or service	Says what the feature will do	Gives the value of worth that the buyer will get from the product or service
'Because (of) . . .'	'You can . . .'	'Which means that . . .'

The following exercises will help you to develop benefit statements for yourself.

Identifying benefits for a product/service

Choose something that you have bought recently. Write down four features in the 'Feature' column below. Now turn each feature into advantages and benefits (one feature can often give rise to a large number of benefits).

Feature: what it is	Advantage: what it does	Benefit
Because (of) . . .	You can . . .	Which means that . . .

Identifying benefits for me

Identify four of your achievements that you are proud of and write them in the 'Feature' columns. Convert your features to advantages and benefits for your target job.

Feature: What have I done? What are my achievements?	Advantage: What I will be able to do	Benefit: What it means to you
Because (of) . . .	You/I can . . .	Which means that . . .

At the end of each statement ask yourself 'So what?' to challenge the relevance of what you say to the recruiter.

CHAPTER TWENTY-SIX

How to be a better listener

Don't miss a thing

'He who talks much cannot talk well.'

Carlo Goldoni

Most of us are poor listeners . . . 'Sorry, did you say something?' I said most of us are poor listeners!

We are so concerned with what we are going to ask or say that we ignore or miss a lot of what the other person says.

Improving your active listening skills will help you to collect valuable information in your research interviews, when you're networking and when you are being interviewed for a job.

Stages in a networking interview

1 Establish a relationship.

2 Encourage the other person to talk.

3 Reflect what the other person has said.

4 Summarise the key ideas you have got from the meeting.

5 Thank them for their time.

Look at the ten commandments of active listening below. How many 'sins' did you commit in your last networking interview?

The Ten Commandments of Active Listening

1 Judgement evaluation – thou shalt not judge or evaluate until thou hast understood!

2 Non-critical inference – thou shalt not infer thoughts, facts or ideas in addition to those stated; avoid embellishment!

3 Plural inference – thou shalt not attribute thine own thoughts and ideas to the speaker!

4 Lack of attention – thou shalt not permit thy thoughts to stray nor thine attention to wander!

5 Attitude – thou shalt not close thy mind to others!

6 Wishful hearing – thou shalt not permit thy heart to rule thy mind!

7 Semantics – thou shalt not interpret words and phrases except as they are interpreted by the speaker!

8 Excessive talking – thou shalt not become infatuated with the sound of thine own voice!

9 Lack of humility – thou shalt not consider thyself too good to learn from any person!

10 Fear – thou shalt not fear improvement, correction or change!

Improving your listening skills

Non-verbal listening skills

You can communicate that you are listening actively by showing that you are paying full attention and not just waiting for your turn to speak. For example, by:

- looking at the person
- nodding your head
- facial expressions, for example raised eyebrows or a smile
- attentive body posture, for example sitting forward.

Verbal listening skills

There are a number of ways which will indicate clearly not only that you are listening but also interested in what the other person has to say.

- Rephrasing in your own words, for example 'So what you are saying is . . .'
- Summarising key points.
- Encouraging the other person to continue, for example 'That's interesting, tell me more.'
- Asking questions for further information or clarification, for example:
  Why do you say that?
  Why is that important to you?
  What do you mean by that?
  What does that mean to you?
  Would you explain that further?
  How does that relate to what you said before?
  Could you give me an example of that?
  Can you define or describe that?

If you remember Rudyard Kipling's reply when he was asked how he came to develop such a wide knowledge, you won't go too far wrong. He said:

> I keep six honest serving men
> (they taught me all I knew);
> Their names are What and Why and When
> And How and Where and Who.

Attitude

The chief requirement for active listening is to have 'room' for others – if we are preoccupied with our own thoughts, ideas and views, we are not mentally 'available' to listen effectively.

When listening, it is really helpful to try to understand the other person's view, without superimposing your own views or judgements prematurely – a major block to active listening.

Back to 'the ten commandments of active listening'!

CHAPTER TWENTY-SEVEN

How to create a positive image

Impact through body language and dress

'There is new strength, repose of mind and inspiration in fresh apparel.'

Ella Wheeler Wilcox

When we communicate with people in a face-to-face setting we use two principal ways to transmit our message – words (content and voice tone) and body language.

- The 'word message' is made up of the words spoken and the way the words are spoken.
- The 'body language message' is the message we project through our gestures, actions and the way we dress.

Now, interviews are all about talking, usually one-to-one with another person, aren't they? You would be forgiven, then, for thinking that when you first meet someone you are going to capture their attention, provided that you have something interesting to talk about! It may surprise you to know that a number of studies have shown that the majority (around 80 per cent) of the messages we transmit to other people are through our body language.

We have spent a good deal of time so far in this book concentrating on what should be said in interviews. In this chapter we will look at techniques you can use so that your body language projects the impression that you would want it to project.

Stereotypes

Whether you like it or not, most people label others within the first few moments of meeting. As much as 90 per cent of a person's impression of you is made in the first four minutes. Some of your initial impact comes from what you say but the majority comes from the way you behave and the way you dress – the other person stereotypes you.

To give you an example. In most western films what does the 'bad guy' look like? Moustache/unshaven, dark/black clothing and a black hat. He is easy to recognise – Lee Van Cleef hasn't played the part of a schoolteacher or parish priest, as far as I can remember, neither has Tommy Lee Jones!

In the classic western, Butch Cassidy and the Sundance Kid confused our stereotyping by wearing camel-coloured clothes and being fresh-faced and clean-shaven (the slightly more villainous one wore a moustache). By breaking the stereotype, two outright criminals endeared themselves to millions of viewers.

Speak to most rational people and they will argue quite strongly that they 'always keep an open mind when they meet new people' and that they are 'never quick to form an opinion'.

I understand the sentiment. In reality, I'm afraid it's not true.

Try this. Quickly imagine:

a secretary	now
a plumber	now
a school-meals assistant	now

What was each person wearing? Was the secretary clean-shaven, or did he have a beard or moustache? Was the plumber wearing a dress or a skirt? Was the school-meals assistant wearing a jacket, or was he wearing a sweater? Were you guilty of stereotyping?

You will stand a far better chance of getting the job you want if the image you project, through your dress and body language, creates the right impact – in those vital first four minutes. You need to show that you fit into the stereotype.

Now I know that some people are very uncomfortable with what I have just said, and are probably ready to throw this book in the bin . . . 'What about freedom of choice?' . . . 'No, I'm afraid what they see is what they get' . . . 'If they don't like me as I am then I'd rather go elsewhere.' If this is the way you feel then fine, I respect your opinions. What I will say, however, is that you are almost certainly shortening your options.

My target job

What is your stereotype of someone doing your target job? How do they look? How are they dressed? What does their body language say? Make a few notes here.

_____

_____

_____

Positive impact – body language

If you are male dress yourself in a dark blue pinstriped suit, a white cotton shirt with double cuffs, a 'military' striped tie, black lace-up shoes and wear a plain-faced watch. The female equivalent is the same with no tie, a white cotton blouse and black court shoes. Your body language is about as persuasive and influential as your dress can let you be (We'll call this No. 5 dress).

Some years ago, studies carried out by IBM found that people dressed as I have just described were 40 per cent more believable than those who were 'less powerfully' dressed.

The less believable end of the scale is the camel-coloured suit, brown shoes and coloured shirt (No. 1 dress). While higher up come the light greys (No. 2 dress) with dark greys even higher (No. 4 dress). Watch the politicians and other public figures on television to assess what effect their dress has on their 'believability quotient' with you.

It is impossible to generalise and give a definitive 'this is what you should wear for interviews', since all jobs have different requirements. In addition, as organisations evolve 'casual cultures' and flexible working patterns emerge making it almost impossible to be definitive. The finance director of one company may wear a dark blue No. 5 suit while their counterpart in another organisation may go to work in T-shirt, jeans and trainers. Whatever is appropriate to the culture, you can't go wrong if you're neat, clean and well groomed. Here are some general principles.

- Decide where, on the 1–5 scale, your dress should be appropriate to the job. Lovely as that new suit is (you know, the one you bought for your brother's wedding), ask yourself if it is right for the job interview.

- Clean, well-pressed clothes in good repair – there aren't any buttons missing from the shirt/blouse you're planning to wear are there?

- Wear some perfume or aftershave – but make sure it's not too overpowering. Be subtle.

- If you keep pets, brush your clothes thoroughly – those cat hairs will start to look three feet long if you spot them on your clothes in the middle of an interview!

- Polish your shoes until you can see your face in them – not suede ones!

- If you're carrying a briefcase give it a polish.

- For men – earrings and white socks are a turn-off for most recruiters.

- For women – if you're wearing a new skirt, try the sit-down test when you buy it; is it too short? I once interviewed a young woman who sat through the whole process with her top coat on her lap. She'd bought a new skirt for the interview and only realised how short it was when she sat down in it for the first time on the bus, on the way to the interview – too late!

- Beware of silk shirts and blouses – perspiration can really spoil their smart appearance.

- If you wear nail polish use neutral colours.

- If you wear jewellery ask yourself if it is appropriate or too loud.

- Carry a spare pair of stockings/tights in your bag.

- Take only one bag with you into the interview. Fumbling between a handbag and a briefcase can make you look disorganised and reduces your confidence.

- A number of my friends have benefited from 'having their colours done' by taking advice on colours and tones to suit their skin and hair colour. The downside is that it's quite expensive – you may need to change your wardrobe! The positive side is that most of them feel it was beneficial.

If you are leaving education, returning to work after a career break, switching career – such as leaving the armed forces or the police – or making any career step that takes you into a new work culture, it really is worth giving careful thought to the image you want to project. You may need to make a 'transformational' image change to give yourself the best chance.

In addition to standing tall, smiling and being warm and friendly towards interviewers, the following will help you to send out positive messages.

- A handshake: rightly or wrongly, people read all kinds of interpretations into people's handshakes, from the limp lettuce non-assertive to the knuckle-crushing bully! A firm but gently 'middle ground' handshake is usually appropriate to start and end interviews.
- Don't crowd the interviewer's personal space – in western society 4–6 feet is about as near as you should get to someone in an interview.
- Hold eye contact – but don't stare.
- Mirror the interviewer's body gestures – if the interviewer crosses their legs, do the same. If they raise their hand to their face, copy their gesture to produce a 'mirror image'. You are telling the interviewer that you are in agreement with their ideas or attitudes. Make sure that your mirroring is natural, otherwise it will look like mimicking! If you want to observe mirroring, go along to your local pub and watch people making each other feel relaxed by mirroring.
- Don't sit with your arms crossed – they form a physical block or barrier and send out an 'I don't believe you' message.

Read the other person's body language:

- Pulling or poking their ear – they've heard enough. Move on.
- Hand clenching or clenching the chair arm – they're not impressed with your answer. Change the subject.

- Readjusting their cuff/watch strap – they're bored. Move on.
- Sitting back – they want to listen.
- Leaning back with hands clasped behind the head – they want you to convince them.
- Rubbing the chin suddenly – they're interested in what you're saying.
- Index finger pointing up and resting on the cheek – they're evaluating what you're saying.
- Leaning forward and rubbing hands together – they're very interested in what you're saying.

Last impressions

A last impression from me!

Don't get so 'hung up' about gestures, actions and dress that you forget about the content of the interview! Watch people in real life or on television for examples of what I'm talking about.

When you attend an interview, a few well-chosen gestures and nicely matched attire will help you to create that perfect impression in the first four minutes.

Your way in: finding vacancies

Reactive and proactive jobsearching

'The sleeping fox catches no poultry'

Benjamin Franklin

There are three kinds of job vacancies. Those which:

- already exist – someone has been promoted or left, etc.
- are about to exist – as a result of retirement or someone moving on or a company expansion
- are created – because your approach convinces the employer that there is a problem to be solved.

There are two ways of job searching

- **Reactive** – you read the vacancies sections in newspapers, journals and the vacancy boards of the job centre. Estimates vary, but many believe that as few as 25 per cent of all job vacancies are ever advertised.
- **Proactive** – you combine your investigative and entrepreneurial skills to discover vacancies and market yourself so that you get that job.

Persistence and flexibility pay

When I was a 19 year old student, I borrowed the airfare to the United States and enough money to exist on for 11 weeks from my parents. (Students do get long holidays don't they!) My travelling companion, Keith, and

I arrived in Atlantic City, which is like Blackpool but around ten times bigger, in the middle of the holiday period. We had work permits and were sure that we'd be able to find jobs. We couldn't. American students start their summer holidays before the UK colleges. Every temporary job had gone. We spent three full days from 7.00 am until 10.00 pm calling at every hotel, restaurant, shop . . . anywhere where we thought we could get work.

We took a bus to Philadelphia and spent another day doing the same thing there. But no luck.

We took a bus to Harrisburg. By mid-afternoon we had met a clerk at the employment offices who said there were no jobs in Harrisburg, but if we were interested in picking fruit he would take us that night to Gettysburg, where he knew there were jobs.

At 7.00 am the next morning we waited for the bus to arrive to take us to the fruit farm. It didn't arrive. It had been cancelled. No jobs.

The Gettysburg address I had was 3000 miles from home – we knew no one else and had just about enough money to survive for the rest of the trip! Back to knocking on doors. We also wrote a letter to the editor of the local newspaper saying how much we were enjoying our visit to the USA, but did anyone have any work?

In the meantime I managed to get a job – as a dishwasher at a Holiday Inn. Two days later our letter was published and a director of a shoe factory (who was English) rang to offer us jobs. Promotion! I resigned my job as a dish-washer and started at the shoe factory.

Two days after that, I received a call from a Howard Johnson restaurant asking if I wanted a job as a cook. I explained that I had a daytime job but was available during the evenings and at weekends. I started that evening.

I now had two jobs. A week later one of the other cooks resigned. I told the manager that Keith was available. He now had two jobs.

Persistence, flexibility, creativity and networking took the pair of us from being unemployed to having jobs that earned us enough money to repay our debts, finance our flights and an 11-week stay, which included a three-week, 11,000-mile tour of the USA!

Reading the appointments section in newspapers is an important part of jobsearching but there are many other ways.

Proactive job searching

And there are two ways of proactive jobsearching!

Traditional techniques of proactive jobsearching

- Identify potential employers and write to a named person – not the personnel manager (unless you're looking for a personnel job) but the person running the department.
- To help in identifying potential employers take a trip to your local library and do some book research. There are literally dozens of directories. A quick phone call can confirm a name. When you know which geographical area, industry/public sector you are targeting, ask the librarian for advice on which directories will be most useful. The books will be in the reference section and some of the titles you will find useful will be:

  The Personnel Manager's Year Book

  Kompass Register of British Industry and Commerce

  Who Own Whom? – *A directory published by AP Information Services (see: www.apinfo.co.uk)*

  Stock Exchange Official Year Book

  Directory of British Associations

  Kelly's Manufacturers and Merchants Directories (regionalised).

  And don't forget the Yellow Pages and other local directories. And also the membership lists of professional bodies, for example the Institute of Chartered Accountants in England and Wales, the Law Society, the Institute of Taxation, etc. There are also industry-specific directories. The list goes on and on – don't be put off. Ask for help and be prepared to do some digging!

- Write speculative letters and e-mails to headhunters and recruitment agencies. Build up your bank of names and addresses from friends and business contacts. Also, scan the newspapers and journals (current and previous editions) for people who work in your target area. An excellent source of names and addresses is the *CEPEC Recruitment Guide*.

- Contact the branch chairperson or secretary of your professional organisation.

- Network – first of all, brainstorm the names of as many friends, acquaintances and business contacts as you can. Telephone them and get to the point quickly. Have three objectives:

  - To let them know that you're looking for work – so that they can keep their eyes and ears open

  - To ask them for the names of two of their contacts you might approach

  - To ask for their advice about opportunities/recruitment consultants/ journals/ads they might have seen.

- Personal recommendation – if you have been made redundant, will your previous manager write to, or telephone, or e-mail people in their network to ask if they will meet you? . . . Ask!

GOYA techniques of proactive jobsearching

Get off your a***!

- Be prepared to put in **a lot of effort** – whatever effort you have planned to put into jobsearching, double it to a minimum of 20 hours per week and be prepared for a long journey. You need to put in some long hours. Be prepared to make dozens of phone calls and be prepared to write tens, or even hundreds, of letters of application.

- Target small companies – with a few exceptions, the big companies are contracting while some of the smaller ones are growing. Also, in a smaller company you're far more likely to get to see the decision-maker. Go there in person.

- Go to visit potential employers – arrive in reception, ask for the manager by name and be ready for a short interview. This is what salespeople call a speculative call – of course it doesn't work every time. In fact to be realistic it won't work most of the time. But if you never do it, then it won't ever work. And you only need it to really work once, don't you? Be brave, try it! Remember what I said earlier about 'the glass is always full'!

- Set yourself a target to see five employers each week – either through formal interviews or through speculative calls as described above.

- Visit your old school, college or university, nursing school, etc. – people there may be aware of vacancies for people with the skills or knowledge you have, or they may be able to give you names to add to your network.

- Have lots of 'irons in the fire' – sometimes when people are jobsearching they 'fall in love' with one vacancy. As the interview process proceeds, they exclude any activity in looking for alternatives. It's almost as if there would be some kind of disloyalty to this potential job.

- Network in person – wherever possible meet people face-to-face, rather than on the telephone or by e-mailing each other. They may meet for a quick lunch, a meeting in the pub after work, or for a coffee. They'll give you ten times as much information in a one-to-one meeting as they would in a telephone call or e-mail exchange.

- If you've been shortlisted for a job and are attending a series of interviews put your heart and soul into it – but don't do it to the exclusion of all other activities. Keep jobsearching.

- Be creative, brainstorm – try to think of novel and different techniques of finding out about new jobs. See if your friends can come up with different ways.

Can't be done – don't close your mind! Someone once looked up my name and hand-delivered a nicely packaged box to the reception area of the company, where I worked as a personnel manager. The package was endorsed 'perishable – urgent'. It was delivered to me immediately, straight into my office (not buried in an in-tray) and placed on my desk. The contents – two packs of sandwiches from Marks & Spencer, a can of fresh orange juice, a cream cake and even a napkin. A letter in the box, from a young woman, explained that she realised I was a busy person – perhaps if she bought me lunch then the time I had saved could be spent giving her a short interview? When she telephoned me two days later, I spoke to her personally and met her a few days later. She had jumped in front of literally dozens of people. Regrettably, we didn't have any suitable vacancies. If we had, she would have been near the front of the queue . . . no, not because she bought lunch for me but because she was prepared to try something different! It nearly worked. What she did get were some contact names of people in my network.

PS: I'm not suggesting that you now start to feed every potential recruiter! I am simply trying to demonstrate that there are merits in thinking creatively.

Here's another example of determination reaping its rewards. It was given to me by friend of mine who is a partner in a law firm.

'When recruiting for a solicitor we used a headhunter, found an ideal candidate and he turned us down. Then I went to specialist agencies. Lots of CVs, interviews, etc. I turned down one person – not convinced she could develop the business enough. She wrote to me a couple of days later with her ideas for generating further business. I was impressed, had her back for a further interview and she got the job!'

If you have an interesting jobsearch method you have used, which has worked, write to me or e-mail me at the address given at the end of the book, so that we can share it with your fellow jobsearchers.

You may be asking yourself *'Which jobsearching technique should I use?'*

My advice is ALL OF THEM.

Finding your job on the Net

Finding a job using the World Wide Web

'The expectations of life depend on diligence; the carpenter that would perfect his work must first sharpen his tools.'

Confucius

Since I wrote the first edition of this book the Internet has permeated many aspects of our lives. It's a playground, a shopping mall, the best library in the world and the quickest (and cheapest) way of obtaining and sending information that I know. E-commerce, the use of the Internet in business, has well and truly come of age and it's still evolving. Very soon you will be able to drive to a new town and ask your on-board computer something like who needs a personnel manager in this area? And, hey presto, there will be a list of local vacancies! Whether we need it or not it will soon be here. But for the moment, let's concentrate on the here and now and look at the Internet.

'It is not necessary to use the Internet if you are looking for a job. But not using it says three things about you. The first is that you have not yet grasped the importance of the Internet as a tool for accessing information. Second, you are restricting your career plans to people and places you are already familiar with. Third you are an ageing dinosaur crippled by technofear.'

Tony Glover, writing in MicroScope, an IT journal

Ouch! That hurts, but he's right. You CAN get a job without using the Internet and many do, but using the Net in your jobsearch strategy you'll increase your chances of success. Some of the best sites have information exchange communities, careers advice and career-planning resources so that you can conduct your jobsearch from one site.

As an experiment, I have just used the *Times Educational Supplement* website to check for teaching jobs in Lincolnshire. Within less than two minutes I had an up-to-date list of vacancies! The power of the Internet in jobsearching gets even better!

Imagine being able to go to bed at night, and when you go back to your desk the next day your own private army of researchers has scoured trade publications, newspapers and journals. They have also phoned a few thousand recruitment agencies and employers to find jobs that would be of interest to you. Sitting neatly on your desk is a small, but perfect, pile of 'ideal job' vacancies! Well, your dreams have come true. Don't ask me how it works but the best sites have this facility.

When you register with them you can set up a process in which their computer will automatically search their database each day to see if any new jobs match your criteria. You then receive an e-mail to notify you of the new job! To test the process I registered with *www.monster.co.uk* and inputted my search criteria to my own jobsearch 'agent' two months ago. Since then, I have received notification of new jobs almost daily! What could be easier? There's no cost, so even if you're not actively looking for a job, you can sign up your 'search agents' and get e-mails to keep your finger on the pulse of the job market.

But how do you get the best out of using the Internet in your jobsearch? Well, as the old expression goes the best way to learn how to play the flute is to play the flute! But before you go online read what the experts have to say.

The Internet has made such a significant impact on recruitment that I thought it would be useful to get the views of people who work in the field on a day-to-day basis. I am therefore extremely grateful to Professor Dave Bartram of SHL plc, Simon Parker at Monster.co.uk and Andrew Banks and Geoff Morgan for the following contributions. If you're new to the Net, their guidance should help you to understand just how important, and useful, effective use of the Internet can be. (SHL plc advise over 5,500 client companies worldwide on recruitment and development of their staff. Monster is the leading Internet website for jobsearchers. Andrew Banks and Geoff Morgan are both international experts on this subject.) PS. Web, Net and Internet all mean the same thing.

Using the Net to succeed in your job search

With thanks to Simon Parker, Marketing Director, monster.co.uk.

Ideally, you want your jobsearch to take as little time and energy as possible, while producing optimum results. Sound impossible? It's not, especially if you use the Net to its best advantage.

The ideal job search

The most successful jobsearch is a multifaceted one. You want to achieve the right balance between research, preparation and action, while drawing from a mix of resources. Get it right and you'll expend less energy and vastly increase your chances of finding the right job that matches your needs and skills, and allows you to grow professionally.

If you embark on a traditional jobsearch campaign, you may devote an excessive amount of time and effort that produces little reward. If your only jobsearching activity is checking the classified listings and sending your CV to loads of organisations, you'll probably find yourself with a handful of interviews, at companies that may not be right for you, and have wasted a lot of time. By the same token you can greatly increase your chances by expanding your professional network, researching companies and targeting organisations that are a good fit for your skills, interests and experience. Happily, in today's world, much of this work can be done on the Net.

What are the benefits of using the Net in career planning? Recently, organisations and individuals have begun creating their own presence on the Net. This means there's an enormous amount of information for you to access. At the same time, too many choices can be overwhelming.

Convenience, flexibility and cost efficiency

You can access the Net at any time of day or night. Having your own computer and Internet access means that you can also conduct a good deal of your jobsearching on your own time scale and in the comfort of your own home. Also, because Net resources are categorised and searchable by keywords, you can broaden or narrow your focus as you choose and access large amounts of information easily and efficiently. Links between and within sites enable you to pick and choose your direction, providing a non-linear approach to information gathering. That means you can navigate multiple sources of information with ease and go directly to the source that most appeals to you. In addition, the Net provides a cost-effective means of accessing information from all over the world about job-related issues. It's relatively cheap (even free at many universities) and the information is free. So what career resources are out there, and how can a job seeker effectively use the Net?

Information and preparation

Businesses, professional and industry associations, career-planning tools, careers fairs, job listings – they're all on the Net, so it makes sense that you should be visiting them.

Many businesses have their own sites where you can find basic background information, an understanding of their role in their industry, a glimpse of the corporate culture, job opportunities, contact information and more. Some sites provide company data on a multitude of organisations; others provide detailed financial information through annual reports. You can look up industry information, trends and job prospects through government sites, professional associations and industry guides. There are a number of employment guides that provide employment statistics, useful articles and links to other job-related sites. The Net is full of directories of careers and jobs fairs, electronic job listings and classifieds that you can search by location and keywords. Regional and relocation information can be found online through local, regional and national sites such as local councils, tourist information offices and government sites. Online magazines also provide this information with searchable directories and reviews of various cities and countries.

Communication and guidance

Since the Internet is a massive network, what better place to do your networking? After all, networking is the single most effective means of finding a job. Whether you want advice, to arrange networking and informational interview opportunities or to respond to an ad or job posting, people around the world are available online through their sites and through e-mail, mailing lists, bulletin boards and Net conferencing. The Net is a friendly place. Because of its interactive nature you can contact business people, non-profit people, career professionals and placement offices, professional associations and special interest groups, fellow students and job seekers, and even employment support groups.

University and college sites

Many university careers offices and placement offices have their own sites online, and they are a great source of career-related information, particularly for students, recent graduates, new jobsearchers, and even career changers. If you're a student you can access information from your own university's careers centre, but feel free to visit other university sites as well. These sites generally contain a wealth of information ranging from self-assessment tools to CV and interview preparation tips to campus interview schedules to job listings. Most also offer descriptions of other worthy career-related sites and provide links to them.

Special interest sites

Professional associations and other specialised groups have valuable career-related information. These range from outreach groups, which help to employ particular segments of society – such as women in business – to others that help people with disabilities. There are sites for racial and ethnic groups, for part-time workers and many more. These sites can be excellent for information gathering and networking.

Some self-assessment testing organisations offer their services online to help you evaluate your own skills, interests and values so that you can focus your career goals better.

Advice and insider information

Professional associations and career specialists are online all over the world, providing information on employment and particular industries. Most information is already posted online, with other information on request. Online career columns enable you to submit your questions and receive answers online and through e-mail. There are also mailing lists to which you can subscribe that enable you to communicate with a large number of people, all of whom are interested in the same subject as you and some of whom are experts in the field. You can subscribe to one or more of these to ask questions, increase your network, or even just to be a 'fly on the wall' and observe what's going on in your field of interest. You can also participate in Net conferences and post your requests, questions, concerns, CVs, job postings and more on electronic bulletin boards, and people will respond, sometimes even directly to you.

To get the best out of the Net

Know thyself – do some self-exploration on the Net

Consult self-assessment resources, career and placement centres; read and conduct informational interviews; seek advice through professional associations, e-mail, bulletin boards and mailing lists. Many of these resources can also help you develop important career-planning and jobsearching skills such as writing CVs and covering letters, preparing for interviews, and learning appropriate business terminology and etiquette for different professions.

Know thy target – gather company, industry and regional information

Discover viable occupations and industries that match your skills through government sites, industry sites and online careers magazines that offer detailed descriptions of different professions through articles, statistics and searchable databases. Explore employment possibilities and quality-of-life information for a given city or country by searching government, travel and relocation-related sites. Research prospective target organisations by accessing company home pages and searching company databases.

Make contact

Locate career, business and industry professionals through their respective websites, e-mail, bulletin boards and mailing lists. You can learn more about their businesses and your options, increase your network and pursue job leads. Go forth and conquer!

The final key to enhancing your jobsearch is striking the balance between being inquisitive and efficient in your research. One of the most rewarding aspects of using the Net is mastering its exploration. Be systematic, and don't be daunted. Just remember that the information is out there waiting for you, and it's important to strike a balance between setting your agenda and sticking to it, while still allowing yourself to take advantage of the unknown prize lurking behind Link Number Three. Good luck in your search!

Maximising your use of the Net in your job search

With thanks to Andrew Banks and Geoff Morgan, executive resourcing experts.

The online world is rapidly becoming the easiest way to search and apply for jobs 24 hours a day, seven days a week, without geographic or time barriers.

As the Internet and online population is now greater than the population of many countries, employers and employees alike are flocking to online recruitment and networking.

Building a CV

The reason recruiters and many employers want to receive your CV electronically is because they will store your details electronically in a candidate database. This allows them to search and match your skills against the positions they have vacant instantly.

There are a few basic rules to remember when building an electronic CV.

- Always create as plain text or ASCII, (if the employer only has Word version 3 and you create a Word version 6 file, the employer will not be able to open it.)

- Do not underline headings.
- Do not use italics unnecessarily.
- Do not use tables unnecessarily.
- Always format in portrait style.
- Do not include graphics or photographs of yourself.

If this seems too complicated there are some websites that offer CV-building facilities. These services should always be free of charge. They are designed to assist you to build a professional online CV that is user-friendly, highlights keywords and is in a format that is accepted by almost all employers. The one exception to this rule is government organisations, where you are usually expected to fill out a standard government online application.

The don'ts of on-line jobsearch

- Don't send a general CV without a covering letter stating where and when you are available for work and, most important, what type of job you are seeking.
- Don't send your CV by e-mail to multiple organisations. Remember, the top of every e-mail you send will show who else you sent your details to. Mass e-mails do not create a good impression.
- Don't ask general questions like 'How do I get a job?' or 'Do you have job vacancies?'. Be more specific and remember that yours may be one of thousands of e-mails that an organisation receives weekly. The more specific your question the more specific the answer.
- Don't e-mail your CV to a prospective employer or recruitment firm in the latest Word version. Often the most basic is best – for example a basic text file (.txt) is likely to be accessible by all versions of computer users. Sending your CV in the latest version of Word may make you think you are technologically up-to-date, but it will simply frustrate the potential employer if they are unable to access your document. And it won't do much for your chances of success.

The dos of electronic applications

- Do use keywords that show you match the position requirements.
- Do keep the CV short and sharp – remember, it is only an initial contact.
- Do put your most important skills at the beginning of the CV.
- Do keep the format of the CV simple.
- Do use only plain fonts – no italics or underline and no borders.
- Do remember to provide your e-mail address and telephone number – the aim is to be contactable, so make sure your e-mail address is correct on your CV.
- Do always keep a hard copy of your CV close at hand for incoming enquiries.

Reasons to use the Net in your jobsearch

- **Free access to information and resources** – with access costs to the Internet becoming more and more competitive, more people are beginning to take advantage of the thousands of free resources and job listings, as well as CV writing tips, interview tips and other career guidance tools.
- **Use keywords to find jobs** – newspapers provide job listings; however, they can require extensive visual scanning. The Internet, by way of contrast, allows you to search job databases using keywords for fast, effective retrieval of jobs.
- **Access to company vacancies** – the majority of large companies now provide a page on their website dedicated to vacancies in their organisation, or provide a direct link to their HR department. Many of these vacancies are company-wide and are not geographically restricted.
- **Networking** – the most important part of getting a job is making contacts and where best to do so than on the world's largest electronic network!
- **Tomorrow's information today** – while newspapers publish a job section on a weekly basis, and the information published is only valid on the day of print, the Internet provides you with daily updates of vacancies worldwide.

- **No boundaries!** – the Internet has no geographic or time barriers, and access is available 24 hours a day, 365 days a year.

- **Leading-edge skills** – organisations, especially businesses, are rushing to get onto the Internet. They see opportunities for advertising, possible commercial markets and a vast wealth of information that they can tap into. Using the Internet in your jobsearch demonstrates to the employer your familiarity and skill with this new market area.

- **Searching for jobs using global technology** – there is more to searching for a job on the Internet than giving it to a large online job bank/employment page. You need to have a plan of attack. There are some specific job-related web pages on the Internet that you can use to source the job you are looking for. These are as follows.

  - *Recruitment websites* – a home page for a recruitment firm will display general or industry-specific jobs for you to view. A recruitment website of merit will provide you with the ability to apply for positions online.

  - *Employment jobs bank* – an employment jobs bank represents a site on the Internet where both recruitment firms and employers can post job vacancies. A common service provided by some jobs banks allows you to post your CV in a secure area, so only employers and recruitment firms of your choice can view your details.

  - *Online classified* – an online classified website is what we refer to as a newspaper online. Many of the major newspapers now sport their own website displaying employment adverts that they have printed in the press. If you apply to a classified website your CV will normally be directed to the recruitment firm or employer who has placed that particular vacancy.

  - *Company home pages.*

  - *Electronic journals* – electronic journals are industry-based publications normally managed by a society or organisation. These are usually free and provide industry-related articles and possible networking contacts together with job listings.

  - *Newsgroups* – internet newsgroups are public bulletin boards where you are free to post requests for employment or vacancies. The jobs newsgroups have jobs, CVs, discussions on how to find a job and general career information. Industry-specific news groups provide an excellent opportunity for networking. (For a comprehensive list of newsgroups go to *www.listz.com*.)

- *Mailing lists* – similar to newsgroups, mailing lists cover a broad variety of topics and industries. Occasionally, job postings can be found. However, their main benefit is to establish networking contacts, keep abreast of industry trends and receive updates on who's who in a specific industry.

- **Search engines** – enter keywords, use subject categories, assess recruitment sites through banner advertising.

PEOPLE PERFORMANCE

Internet recruitment, our ally

With thanks to Professor Dave Bartram, Head of Research, SHL Group Plc

Looking for a job can be challenging, finding the right job can be formidable. The key question is, 'How can we, in this rapidly changing world, make some sensible career decisions?' In today's increasingly competitive world, the era of self-managed careers is upon us. It is our future, no one else's, and the answer to the question, to a large extent, lies in our own hands, and, surprisingly, the Internet.

Internet statistics demonstrate why it is so influential – figures from the 2004 National Online Recruitment Audience Survey (NORAS) show that 59% of people in the UK have obtained an interview for a job advertised online. (Electronic Publishing Service, statistics file January 2004: *www.epsltd.com/clients/statistics.asp*)

Today's Internet recruitment and selection sites help our career management in two key areas.

First, our prospective employer is able to provide much more information than has previously been made available through more traditional means, about their organisation, the jobs on offer and, importantly, the organisation's culture and values, issues that are becoming an increasingly important component of the person/job match equation. While on the face of it a similar job title in two organisations may seem the same, in reality the jobs can be radically different when organisational culture and values are taken into account, and may well need contrasting attributes for success in the roles. To take advantage of this opportunity, an essential start point of our career management is to understand our values, so we are able to map them onto those of the organisation to which we are thinking of applying, in effect creating our own shortlist.

The second opportunity that the Internet brings is for us to gain self-insight. While there are many sites that are purely CV-registration sites, there are a growing number that, having encouraged us to apply, then invite us to complete an application form online. Not only do they seek biograph-ical data, they also seek to gain information about our strengths and limi-tations against competencies (behaviours that lead to success in a role). You may be asked to supply this information either by means of free text boxes or by multiple-choice answers to a short questionnaire, or a combi-nation of both. The questions will (or should) have been clearly validated and relate to the demands of the job for which we are applying.

The advantage to us is that the information is being gathered, and sifted, about all applicants in the same standardised manner, which in turn will lead to fairer consideration of our application. Clearly, we need to be able to give examples of experiences against various competencies (for example leadership, teamwork).

Sites are already emerging that include online psychometric assessment. These may be ability tests, personality questionnaires, motivation question-naires – instruments that are in common use already. Such sites have the facil-ity to incorporate a feedback mechanism that will give us information about our strengths and limitations very early in the selection process – a true source of self-insight to aid self-selection. How should we answer the questions? Just as we would with pencil and paper questionnaires – openly and honestly.

'There will be many opportunities throughout our working life for us to push back the frontiers of self-knowledge. The Internet is one. We should fear none, but grasp each one with relish. Sometimes it takes two or more people to really know one.'

Nowack, 1993

Are you ready to stand naked in the street?

Now you have read the experts' advice, some words of caution. Let me ask – would you stand naked in the centre of your local city, shouting to the world that you're looking for a new job carrying a placard displaying your address, phone number, earnings, medical history, age and sex of your children, etc.? No, I didn't think you would! Watch out that you don't do the electronic equivalent on the Net. Internet users reflect society and while most people are honest and decent, some are not. Beware of what you tell to whom. Whilst there are a number of professional bodies in the UK for people who work in recruitment, there is *no statutory regulatory body*. This means that, quite literally, anyone can register a recruitment website address, and upload their website onto the Net in less than 24 hours. (It is illegal for them to advertise jobs that don't exist however.) Do tread cautiously on the Net – once you have given out information, you can't get it back! Check out the credibility of Internet recruiters and don't reveal personal details in chatrooms, communities and newsgroups.

www.Get-That-Job.co.uk

The website of *Get That Job!* is *www.Get-That-Job.co.uk* and is dedicated to helping you in your jobsearch.

There are many thousands of recruitment sites now available on the Internet, and the number is growing daily! I've spent many, many days trawling the Net and have compiled a number of specialist directories which link to the best recruitment and career development websites to help you to 'hit the ground running' in your Internet jobsearch. You'll also find links to all of the other books that I have referred to while you've been reading.

If you're eager to get started, here are ten good quality sites. But don't forget to pay us a visit at *www.Get-That-Job.co.uk*

- *www.londonjobs.co.uk* – the (London) *Evening Standard*'s jobsite
- *www.pearsoned.co.uk/bookshop/minds/gradcareers* – FT Prentice Hall's excellent site for graduates

- *www.careersolutions.co.uk* – careers advice, books and software
- *www.gisajob.com* – jobs and links to employment agencies
- *www.jobsearch.co.uk* – scans your CV and target job, and searches for you
- *www.jobsite.co.uk* – a site from UK and European recruitment agencies
- *www.monster.co.uk* – leading site for jobs, advice and newsgroups
- *www.stepstone.co.uk* – UK and European, job vacancies in many sectors
- *www.totaljobs.com* – UK site and jobs worldwide with free salary checker
- *www.workthing.co.uk* – UK site and jobs worldwide

Some final thoughts

The rate of change of modern technology means that some recruiters, like many other people, will continue to explore new possibilities. A friend of mine from the UK was interviewed by webcam on the Internet for a job in Australia. The images were jumpy but this was acceptable compared with the cost of flights (she got the job!). I'm told that as more bandwidth becomes available high quality video streaming will become commonplace. Translated into English I understand that this means that (probably by the time this book leaves the printers!) if you've got a webcam linked to a computer connected to the Internet, recruiters will be able to interview you across the Internet. You'll be able to attend four or five interviews a day without leaving home!

Don't be daunted by the new technology! Remember, all these new methods used by recruiters are nothing more than tools to help them to make the best decision. They are not an end in themselves. And for the foreseeable future, I believe, interviews in person will continue to be our most popular selection method.

Whatever selection methods you encounter, the most important thing to remember is that the recruiter is recruiting a person. Decide what you want out of life. Identify the career and find the job that fits your career and life plans. And when you get to the selection process, let the power of your personality persuade them that you are that person!

I believe that the Internet is the most significant technological development of modern times. Seize its power, grab your mouse and go surfing!

CHAPTER THIRTY

How recruiters pick candidates

The recruiter's shopping list

'Nothing is really work unless you would rather be doing something else.'

James Matthew Barrie

Present yourself well in an interview and you're probably 95 per cent of the way to getting the job! So, how do you do it? We'll look at recruitment interview questions later, but it's useful to have some insight into how recruiters go about selecting candidates.

Many take a 'hit and miss' approach with little structure. Good interviewers, however, work to a plan, using questions to measure/assess you against their ideal profile. They set standards and requirements relating to a variety of factors and decide if these are essential or desirable. The table on page 217 shows a typical 'person profile form' used by many recruiters.

How the selection criteria are used

When planning a recruitment project, a recruiter will use the 'person profile' like a shopping list to try to help them to identify what the *ideal* candidate should be like. This may seem a little clinical but, if you think about it, it's no different to you sitting down and drawing up a list of criteria for a new family car:

- Must have manual gearbox
- Must have five seats minimum, seven would be ideal
- Prefer aircon, but sunroof is OK
- Must be diesel
- Prefer blue or grey metallic – definitely no bright garish colours!
- Prefer mileage below 25,000 but up to 60,000. OK if it has full main dealer service history

And so it goes on. You can then browse the papers or visit the dealers with your checklist.

It's just the same in recruitment. For example, someone selecting a marketing executive might decide that it is essential that the person should be of graduate level and desirable that they should have an upper second class honours degree. They may decide that it is essential that the person has very good interpersonal skills since they will be working with a variety of people etc. Some information is easy to establish (such as exam grades), while other information (such as interpersonal skills) involves judgement and evaluation of answers given to questions.

The person profile is the recruiter's shopping list to help them to identify the ideal candidate. This is not my list, but is a 'classic list' that is taught to managers and HR professionals worldwide. Of course there are variations. For example it is illegal to discriminate as far as age is concerned in some countries, while in other countries it's perfectly legal. When you are applying for jobs, work out what would be your 'ideal candidate' for the job if you were recruiting. What would you be looking for? Use the 'person profile' as a checklist.

Person profile	Essential	Desirable
Physical make-up – height/build, appearance, health, speech, etc.		
Attainments – education, qualifications, training, work achievements		
General intelligence – ability to sustain a logical argument, common sense, creativity		
Special aptitudes – numeracy, literacy, creativity, mechanical aptitude, dexterity, etc.		
Interests – political, social, active, outdoor, practical, intellectual, etc.		
Disposition – interpersonal relationships, influence over others, industry, self-control, self-reliance, dependability, etc.		
Circumstances – family and domestic, willingness to relocate, willingness to travel, etc.		
Motivation – why this job? – has the person got the 'can do' and 'will do'?		

31

Preparing for your interview

How to succeed

'When you have spoken the word, it reigns over you.
When it is unspoken, you reign over it.'

Arabian proverb

How you can prepare

The FBI says 'proper preparation and practice prevent a poor performance'. Prepare carefully and practise thoroughly for your interview. You will increase your confidence and your chances. Don't rely on charm and wit, there's too much at stake. Interviewers like well-prepared candidates who show a genuine interest.

Find out what you can about the job, the organisation, its products or services. Visit the organisation's website and search Google, or use one of the other search engines, to help you to find out more information. Get a copy of the annual report (if it's a plc or public sector organisation, they have to provide an annual report when requested). Phone the public relations or communications department, or go there in person. Get hold of product literature – getting a youngster to telephone the public relations department for a 'school project' is a good technique if you feel uncomfortable asking (although most people will view it positively if you request additional information). Research into the type of company – public, private, family owned; its performance compared with competitors; etc. Frankly in today's information-rich environment, you may as well not bother turning up for interview if you haven't done some basic research on the Net. Then you need to think about going the extra mile so that you can distinguish yourself from the rest of the pack!

If you can, talk to people who use the organisation's products or services. A friend of mine, Michael, lost his job as a pharmaceutical salesman. He applied for a job selling replacement heart valves. Michael had no experience of selling surgical implants, so he went to the cardiac theatre at a large London teaching hospital, and spoke to some of the surgical team about their use of replacement heart valves. A couple of days later he spent a whole day in an operating theatre seeing the products in use – and all he did was to ask the surgeon whether he could. And yes, he got the job! Now he's the company's managing director in Australia!

Ask for a copy of the job description if one hasn't been supplied with the application information. (A job description is a document that clearly states what your duties will be, your decision-making latitude, and how you will be assessed in the job-performance indicators). If there isn't a job description, ask yourself why not? There may be a perfectly good reason or it may be that they haven't yet decided what your duties will be (a potential source of discontent for the future), or it may well be that the organisation has an informal structure and culture, and your job description may simply be 'whatever is needed to get the job done'.

Re-read the advertisement, the application form (you did remember to keep a copy of it before you sent it?) and your CV. Highlight what you can offer to match their requirements. Bear in mind that when organisations recruit they rarely get a 'hand-in-glove' fit matching their requirements exactly. Your aim is to convince them that you are the *best* match.

Now is the time to cast modesty aside. It is almost certain that you will be asked something like, 'Tell me about yourself' or 'What can you offer to our organisation?'

'Tell me about yourself'

Before the interview, write a short 'You' statement which answers this question. Make five or six positive statements (remember to include benefits) about yourself. Focus especially on your work skills. If you have completed the earlier exercises this step should be straightforward.

Positive statements

I _____

I _____

I _____

I _____

I _____

I _____

Now practise saying it – yes, I know it feels uncomfortable but it is worth it, because it does work.

Practise the interview with a friend who is prepared to give you some feedback. Use a tape recorder, or better still a video camera to hear/see yourself as others do. If you haven't got one and can't borrow one, they are available on hire from many electrical or photographic stores and are often cheaper to rent midweek. Don't be despondent – we are all our own greatest critics and your accent isn't really that noticeable!

Are you up-to-date with developments in your field? – scan the trade journals and the Net. What are the four or five latest innovations / initiatives / developments / trends? What are your opinions of them? You don't have to be a guru to be informed.

Read the day's local newspaper and a national paper, and scan any articles that might be directly related to the organisation. Also make a mental note of the main news stories of the day and formulate a view or opinion.

If you can, find out who will be interviewing you – think about what they might be looking for. This is particularly important if you are applying for a promotion or you already know the organisation well.

Decide an acceptable financial package – but let the interviewer raise it.

Plan your journey. There is virtually no excuse for being late for an interview. Allow extra time for rush-hour traffic, road works and finding a parking space.

Interview day

Dress smartly in well-pressed, comfortable clothes appropriate to the job/organisation. Get your hair trimmed. Do what you can to make yourself feel good – if you feel good inside, you'll present yourself well on the outside.

Arrive early so that you can prepare yourself. Admiral Horatio Nelson is reputed to have said, 'I owe my success in life to always being 15 minutes before my time'. I can't vouch for the accuracy of the statement, but the principle is sound! Don't arrive more than 15 minutes before the interview however – wait outside. Some people view arriving much too early as poor time-management. They may be embarrassed to keep you waiting for a long time.

When you speak with receptionists and secretaries, remember they may be asked for their comments, as may the person who gave you an 'informal' tour of the site or offices before the interview.

Look around – could you work in these conditions, do people seem comfortable talking to each other, what is your impression of the culture? If you prefer a formal working environment where everyone is Mr or Ms, etc. and you hear first names being used the culture may not be right for you, and vice versa.

Leave the raincoat and umbrella in reception, so that you'll arrive at the interview uncluttered.

The interview

Smile and shake hands firmly, if the interviewer offers a hand. Wait to be invited to sit down. If the wait seems too long ask, 'Where would you like me to sit?'

If you're offered a drink, accept it. Even if you only take one or two sips, it will be very useful if your throat starts to dry up.

Remember, you are well on the way to a job offer. The interviewer hopes you're the right person! Take a few deep breaths, relax and be natural. This is your opportunity to show that you are the person they're looking for.

Sit well back into your chair, in an upright but comfortable position. If you use your hands when talking be aware of it and don't overdo it. Make friendly eye contact with the person asking questions. Don't stare. If you feel uncomfortable holding eye contact with people, look at the point of their forehead just above the nose – it works, honestly. If there is more than one interviewer, make sure you also involve them by addressing part of your answer to them. For panel interviews address the main body of an answer to the questioner, but then hold eye contact with other panel members in order to involve them. Only use the interviewer's first name if invited.

Brevity is the essence of good communication. Pause briefly for a second to think before you speak. Don't ramble, wasting valuable time. The interviewer is more interested in the quality of your answer than the quantity! Don't waste too much time talking about your early career, your recent achievements are usually far more relevant.

Listen actively to what is being asked or said – if you need to get a better understanding repeat or rephrase their question.

Be prepared for questions the interviewer knows you'll find difficult to answer, such as ones about a controversial subject. These are asked to see how you respond under pressure. Don't blurt out the answer – a short pause shows thoughtfulness.

Stress what it is about your skills and achievements that makes you the person for the job. Introduce those five or six key 'You' points (page 220) using benefit statements (see also Chapter 25 page 185). Help the interviewer to see how your skills and experience will benefit their organisation. It will be too late if you remember when you're halfway home!

If the interviewer is your potential manager ask yourself whether you will be able to work with him or her.

Have a notepad and pen handy in your bag, pocket or briefcase to take any notes and also to record the answers to your questions at the end of the interview. This shows you have thought about the job. Questions you might like to use are shown near the end of this section. Thank the interviewer and ask about the next step. This confirms your interest in the job.

Avoid:

- Smoking, even if the interviewer does.
- Showing references, job descriptions or samples of your work, unless asked.
- Criticising employers and recounting long stories about why you left jobs, particularly if you have a grievance with a previous employer.
- Talking about personal and domestic matters, unless asked.
- Getting on your soap box. What you do in your own time is of little concern to most employers, but few like activists or shop-floor politicians at work. Practise courteous answers to any likely questions.
- Mentioning salary/package. Let them know what you can do – this may well influence their view of what you are worth. Employers usually have a salary range in mind. If you ask about money too early they will give the lower figure. How many people do you know who have gone shopping to buy, say, a hi-fi system with a price in mind of £500–£650 only to find that they buy one for £725? The same happens in recruitment.
- Name-dropping. It can backfire!
- Interrupting the interviewer in your enthusiasm to make all your points.
- Pretending you've got a better offer elsewhere to try to push them into a decision. But do let them know if you're being interviewed by other people – it can sometimes focus their minds! They don't want to miss out on you but don't give away too much information.

Preparing for their questions

You can't know what is going to be asked but you can improve your chances by practising answering some common questions – ideally with a friend. Start off with 'Tell me about yourself'. (Initial nervousness may cause you to say too much – don't.)

If you're asked to talk about your career history and you've had a variety of jobs, don't dwell on your early career – the interview will have been scheduled for a set time and it is usually more important to talk about current or most recent responsibilities and achievements.

Now try answering some of the questions shown below. Paint the best image of yourself and show what you have to offer by talking about your skills and achievements.

- Why did you leave . . . ?
- How are/were . . . as employers?
- What makes a good employer?
- What have you been doing since you left . . . ?
- What did you enjoy doing at . . . ?
- What are your greatest strengths (weaknesses) as an employee?
- What have been your best achievements?
- What are the qualities needed in a good (job title)?
- What qualities do you look for when recruiting people into your team?
- If we offer you a job, what can you bring to our organisation?
- What area of work do you feel least confident about?
- What do your colleagues/manager see as your greatest weaknesses?
- How would you describe your career progress to date?
- What have you learned in your time with . . . ?
- What do you see yourself doing in 5/10/15 years?
- Why did you become a (job title)?
- How do you take direction?
- How do you spend your holidays?
- Have you ever been dismissed (disciplined)? Tell me about it. (Tell them what you learned from the experience.)
- How is your health?
- How many days sick leave have you taken in the last two years?
- How do you relax?
- What do you know about our company?
- Why do you want this job?
- Why should we offer you this job?
- Are you being interviewed for any other jobs?
- Which do you want?

Some interviewers ask hypothetical questions along the lines of, 'How do you think you would react in . . . situation?' Here you find yourself 'second-guessing' them by saying how you would behave, in the way you think they want to hear! It can become quite an amusing game!

Other interviewers ask questions about what you have done in the past, since this is their best indicator of how you may perform in the future. They are looking for you to have handled situations in a positive way and for you to have learned from experience. Help them by:

- Describing the situation and what had to be done.
- Explaining what you did.
- Describing the outcome in positive terms.

Practise answering some of the questions below. They seem simple but are very searching!

Questions about your effort/initiative

- Tell me about a project you initiated. What prompted you to begin it?
- Give an example of when you did more than was required.
- Give an example of when you worked the hardest and felt the greatest sense of achievement.

Planning and organising skills

- What did you do to get ready for this interview?
- How do you decide priorities in planning your time? Give examples.
- What are your objectives for this year? What are you doing to achieve them? How are you progressing?

Interpersonal skills

- Describe a situation where you wished you'd acted differently with someone at work. What did you do? What happened?
- Can you describe a situation where you found yourself dealing with someone whom you felt was over-sensitive? How did you handle it?

- What unpopular decisions have you made recently ? How did people respond? How did that make you feel?

Sales ability/persuasiveness

- What are some of the best ideas you ever sold a superior/subordinate? What was your approach? Why did it succeed/fail?
- Describe your most satisfying (disappointing) experience in attempting to gain support for an idea or proposal

Decision-making

- What are the most important decisions you have made in the last year? How did you make them? What alternatives did you consider?
- Describe an occasion when you involved others in your decision-making. To what extent did you take notice of their input?

Leadership and teamworking skills

- What are some of the most difficult one-to-one meetings you have had with colleagues? Why were they difficult?
- Have you been a member of a group where two of the members did not work well together? What did you do to get them to do so?
- What do you do to set an example for others?
- How do you work as a team member? Give examples.

Your own questions

Remember that the recruitment interview is a two-way process. You may be making a choice about where you will spend a significant part of your working life. Make the most of your opportunity to find out what you need to know and also to create a business-like impression. Start with questions which show an interest in the job, not what the company can do for you.

Make a note of what you want to ask beforehand. When the interviewer asks if you have any questions, produce your notebook or notepad, and take brief notes of the answers given. Don't think that the interviewer will think you're 'showing off' – quite the opposite. They'll be impressed that you have thought about the job and done some preparation. Examples of information you might like to gather (but not all at once!) are given below.

The job

- What will my daily responsibilities/duties be?
- What is the level of the job within the company's grading structure?
- To whom does the job report?
- Is there a job description/what are the main priorities?
- Reporting – up/down/sideways – are there any dotted-line responsibilities?
- What will be my budget availability?
- What will be my goals/targets/priorities?
- What are relationships like with other departments?
- What are the people like for whom I would be responsible?
- Are there any 'management' issues?
- In what way is the company committed to my training and development?
- What are the opportunities for progress/career advancement?
- What resources would I have available to help me achieve my goals?

The organisation

- What is the UK/total turnover?
- Is there a statement on company philosophy/mission statement?
- What is the company's profitability compared with competitors/budget?
- How big is the workforce/turnover (of staff)?
- What is the range of UK services/products?
- What is the company's e-commerce strategy?
- What new products/services are under development?
- What innovative ways are used to market products/services?
- Where will the organisation be in 5/10 years?

The practicalities

Questions for when you are on the home straight! When considering their offer keep the total package in mind.

- Medical – is it required?
- Start date – how soon?
- Pension – how is the scheme structured? Can you transfer in?
- Salary review – based on what? How often? When will your first one be?
- Car – allocation/running costs or charge?
- Average salary increase last year/previous years? How is it reviewed? Holidays?
- Private healthcare – is it available? How much does it cost? Is spouse/family covered?
- Insurance – what is the company scheme?
- Bonus scheme – what is the structure?
- Share options – are they available?
- Salary – where does the figure they have offered fit in on their salary scales? If they want to start you at the bottom of the scale, ask why and try to convince them that your experience/skills justify being started higher on the scale – see Chapter 36.

Afterwards

Relax and congratulate yourself on having been as well-prepared as you could have been. Reflect on how it went and write down key points which could be important in another interview.

You'll probably have to wait to hear the decision, but you can learn from the experience.

- Were you happy with the way you handled yourself?
- Did you say what you wanted to say?
- Did you find out what you needed to know?
- How many of your 'you' points did you get across?

- Was your behaviour positive, assertive, humble, tense, laid-back, talkative, controlled, etc.?

If you were put forward by a recruitment agency, call them as soon as you can to let them know how you got on and to confirm your interest in the job. They will almost certainly feed this straight back to the interviewer and it will be viewed positively. Otherwise, leave the ball in the court of the interviewer.

Don't become too despondent if you don't hear for a while – recruitment can sometimes take many weeks.

If, however, they have promised to let you know, one way or the other, by a certain date and that comes and goes, there is no harm done by telephoning to see how soon you are going to find out their decision.

Remember that the interviewer is hoping that you are the right person for the job, just as you are hoping to get the job. Do prepare and practise. It will be worth it.

Good luck!

CHAPTER THIRTY-TWO

How to shine in assessment centres

What they are; inside knowledge

'Diligence is the mother of good luck.'

Benjamin Franklin

Assessment centres were first pioneered in the UK by the armed forces and are now used by a number of organisations to select people for jobs. They are very often called 'development centres' when used for internal selection purposes, or to identify fast-trackers and people with potential for promotion. For most candidates it's a once in a lifetime opportunity. Depending on the job, procedures can last from half a day to three days or more.

In the early part of my career I (successfully!) attended a couple of assessment centres as a candidate and since my move into HR management I have run dozens of assessment centres. So I hope the following 'inside information' will be useful. See also the chapters on presentation skills, interview skills and tests and evaluations. The table at the very end of this chapter summarises the exercises at a typical assessment centre and shows how candidates are assessed.

What will happen?

The event will usually be run by a chairperson/facilitator. They will mastermind the whole day and will probably welcome everyone in a group, and say goodbye at the end. They will also run a series of group exercises and tests. They'll also be observing the way everyone works together and be gathering an overview of the 'group dynamics'.

Then there are the observers. They will have been trained and briefed before the meeting. Each observer will be allocated a person or people to observe and they will take copious notes and 'mark' the performance of the candidates. Halfway through the day observers may 'switch candidates' so that a better-balanced view is obtained.

After the assessment centre finishes for you, then the real work of the chairperson and observers begins! The chairperson will now facilitate a process by which each candidate is individually evaluated, against the per-formance standards that were set beforehand. The objective is to try to make the selection process as scientific and as objective as possible. I can tell you from personal experience that these meetings can last a long time, and even into the early hours of the morning!

So how can you outshine the other candidates, and demonstrate that you're the 'best match' for the job?

- Get as much sleep as you can in the days beforehand and try to arrive refreshed. Assessment centres will burn up your adrenalin reserves . . . and more! It's highly likely that, just as you're starting to relax, you'll be handed a mammoth task with a tight deadline to see how you respond under pressure.

- Keep your eyes and ears open and observe the performance of the other candidates. You may be asked to rate their performance. Be prepared to give a factual and analytical summary of their contribution. Don't be afraid of criticising other candidates and don't be afraid of praising them – but make sure it's based on facts. Sometimes you will be given a piece of paper at the end and asked to rank all the candidates (including your-self).

- If you've been invited to join everyone the night before the assessment centre, don't be lulled into a false sense of security by thinking the asses-sors are off-duty. They will probably be assessing your social competence over dinner, in the bar, over breakfast . . .

- Even if you haven't been asked to prepare a presentation, brush up on your skills. There is a good chance that you'll be asked to prepare one at short notice. Pre-select two topics – 'an improvement you've made at work' and an 'interesting angle on your hobby'.

- If you're invited to attend an assessment centre in a hotel, a few casual questions to the manager or receptionist may give you a good idea of what's in store. If the assessors have spent the early part of the day setting up a network of computers in syndicate rooms, then it sounds as if you're going to be involved in a computer-based business simulation. Great fun!

- Try to think through the qualities the assessors will be looking for – leadership, interpersonal skills, ability to handle stress, verbal communication, written communication, flexibility, negotiation skills, problem-solving, business skills, commercial acumen, decision-taking, initiative and creativity. Clearly the weightings will change depending on the job, but commercial acumen, interpersonal communication skills and flexibility must be high on everyone's list.

- Don't try to suppress other candidates in an attempt to make the assessors notice only you. You will come across as overbearing and insensitive.

Assessment centre exercises

Assessment centres are usually designed to include exercises which will measure you against the aspects of the job. **For all of the exercises make sure you understand the chairperson's instructions or the written brief. If you don't understand, ask!**

Not listening and not reading instructions thoroughly are the two biggest causes of frustration in candidates. I have been moaned at, and even shouted at by candidates who had not read instructions properly. Losing your temper and having a go at the chairperson is a career-limiting step, I can tell you! And it does happen – I once sent a candidate home from an assessment centre at lunchtime after she'd lost her temper twice! Remember, you're being tested!

The following are common exercises.

In-tray exercises

You are given the 'in-tray' of a senior manager and have one hour to 'get through it' – otherwise you'll miss your plane! You'll be asked to write on each item what you would do with it, or write a reply to letters, phone messages or e-mails.

- *Quickly* sort the whole pile first and prioritise every item – A (top priority), B and C. They have probably 'buried' some important items, like a resignation of a member of staff, near the bottom!

- Start with the As and work your way through.

- Resignations and other 'people' issues are top priority As.

- Wherever you can, make a note that you would make a telephone call, or send an e-mail – the MD of one of my client companies says that he writes no more than four memos per year.

- If you do write memos, write key messages and let your 'secretary' compose the letter.

- Familiarise yourself with the organisational structure and the briefing instructions before you start, so that you know who's who.

Sales or negotiation role play

You are asked to sell a product or negotiate a deal.

- Ask 'probing' questions – how?, why?, when?, where?, what? and which? are best for gathering information.

- Listen to the answers and try to match the needs of the customer with what the product does! To give an example, one of the all-time favourites when recruiting new salespeople is for the interviewer to say, 'OK sell this fountain pen to me'. Unenlightened candidates immediately start prattling on about style, design, gold nibs and good ink flow. The smart ones ask questions like, 'Do you use a fountain pen?', 'What qualities are important to you when you're choosing a new pen?', 'What would you expect to pay for a fountain pen?'. They then go on to match the product's features and benefits to customer needs.

People who do badly in these exercises do so because they're too busy putting over their own viewpoint, based on assumptions, rather than asking questions to find out what the 'customer' wants!

Business simulation

This may be paper-based or computer-based. You are split into small groups and over a series of rounds, compete to develop, manufacture, market and distribute products. Great fun!

- Play to win!
- Invest in research for new products in the early rounds – products don't last for ever.
- As you get results back at the end of each round analyse the performance of the competitors – you may be able to undercut them or market your product to a niche.

Group discussion (interactive skills)

You are given a problem to solve as a group. Common problems are simulations where your group have been stranded at sea, in the desert or on the moon. (See page 236 for an example of an assessor's form.)

If you're 'stranded' in the desert or on the ocean, being detected is the first priority, followed by food – don't move away to try to save yourself; search parties look for your last location! Try to work out which items you have that can be used as signalling devices.

- Formulate your own ideas quickly and sell them convincingly to the group.
- Suggest that the group needs a structure and timetable to work to – and propose one.
- Don't steamroller other people's ideas, listen attentively.
- If someone isn't contributing, draw them into the group by asking for their ideas.
- Five minutes before the end suggest that you need to summarise your decision and take control, or suggest that someone takes control, of whatever needs to be done.

There are many others types of exercise. For example, if you're applying for a commission in the forces or for other leadership roles, you'll almost certainly be given a series of 'command task' exercises where each person takes a turn at acting as leader. If this is likely to happen, do some reading on leadership skills in advance – I'd recommend *The One Minute Manager* and also *Leadership and the One Minute Manager*, both by Dr Ken Blanchard (whose co-authors were Spencer Johnson on the first and Patricia Zigarmi on the second). If you're applying for a job in marketing you may be asked to write a marketing plan showing how you would launch a new product, or relaunch a failing product. If you're applying for a line management job you might be given an overview (hypothetical or real) of the team you'll be taking over, and the management issues you'll be faced with, and asked to give a short presentation on how you would handle them. Presentations are such an important part of many selection processes these days that I've devoted the whole of the next chapter to how you can prepare for them.

Make the most of your opportunity

An assessment centre is a tremendous opportunity for you to show what you can do. Prepare yourself well and enjoy it. In summary, be positive, be prepared to play the game and project an image of your real self.

INTERACTIVE SKILLS ASSESSMENT

Candidate: ————————————————— Assessor: —————————————

Behaviour	Quality/quantity of contribution	Rating
Giving information		
Seeking information		
Supporting others		
Disagreeing with others		
Persuading others		
Controlling others		
Other contributions		

Comments

Standards

5   Much more than acceptable (significantly above criteria required for successful job performance)

4   More than acceptable (generally exceeds criteria relative to quality and quantity of behaviour required)

3   Acceptable (meets criteria relative to quality and quantity of behaviour required)

2   Less than acceptable (generally does not meet criteria relative to quality and quantity of behaviour required)

1   Much less than acceptable (significantly below criteria required for successful job performance)

Overall rating ————————————————

Selection Panel Assessment Form: Position

Chairperson:

Other panel members:

Interview date:

Exercise

Candidate	Leaderless group	In-tray exercise	Presentation	Marketing plan	1:1 negotiation	Interpersonal /social skills	Interview no. 1	Interview no. 2	Assessment

Panel recommendation:

CHAPTER THIRTY-THREE

How to give a presentation

Prepare, plan, practise, present

'It usually takes me more than three weeks to prepare a good impromptu speech.'

Mark Twain

To assess your self-confidence, ability to communicate and ability to handle a mini-project, some organisations may ask you to make a short presentation, either to a group of managers or, for very senior positions, to the board of directors. Others incorporate a presentation into their assessment centre exercises.

The subject can vary – debating the pros and cons of subjects like e-commerce or mobile comunications, or you may be asked to present a mini-marketing plan for one of the company's products. They may even leave the choice of subject to you. If this happens do not pick 'Where I took my holiday' or 'My hobby'. Do choose a business-related subject that you know something about. The time you are given to prepare can vary from 30 minutes to many days.

If you are asked to give a presentation do take it seriously – management time is very valuable and if the company has gathered an audience to listen to you, then you can be sure that they will be taking it seriously.

Unless you are a natural, or are very experienced, you will probably be nervous. This is a good thing. If you don't have at least some degree of anxiety then you probably aren't taking the exercise seriously.

The keys to an effective presentation are preparation, planning and practice.

Prepare the content

Most people find knowing where to begin is the most difficult step. If you are one of these people I can guarantee the following steps will help you present confidently. *Please*, for the moment, resist any temptation to switch on your PC!

Ask yourself – 'What do I want the audience to learn from my presentation?' Write this objective in the middle of a blank page. Now let your mind 'free-wheel' to produce a mind-map of ideas. The mind-map included here is the one I drew when I started to plan this chapter, which was originally published as an article called 'How to give a presentation and live to tell the tale'.

You'll find that you have far too many things to say, so the next step is to edit and give the presentation some structure.

Choose the most important point you want to communicate. Write it on the presentation planner (there is a blank copy at the very end of this chapter) as key point no. 1. Now add the others in descending order of priority.

Yes, I know that the natural tendency is to save the best to last, but remember that people are most attentive at the start.

Now develop your content by putting the information from your mind-map into your key points. Remember, only information which is relevant to achieving your objectives is allowed. Limit your key points to a maximum of five – three is even better. Think about presenters you admire – are they those who put over a powerful and succinct argument or are they those who waffle and constantly overrun?

You have now developed the main body of your presentation. But before we move on, decide how you will bridge from one point to the next. A phrase like, 'Now let us look at the introduction' lets the listeners know you've finished one topic and gives a signpost to what's next.

Other useful bridges are:

- Enumerating – 'first . . ., second . . ., etc.' when you've stated that you have a specific number of points to cover;
- 'On the contrary' or 'On the other hand' when you're weighing pros and cons, or simply 'Next . . .'.

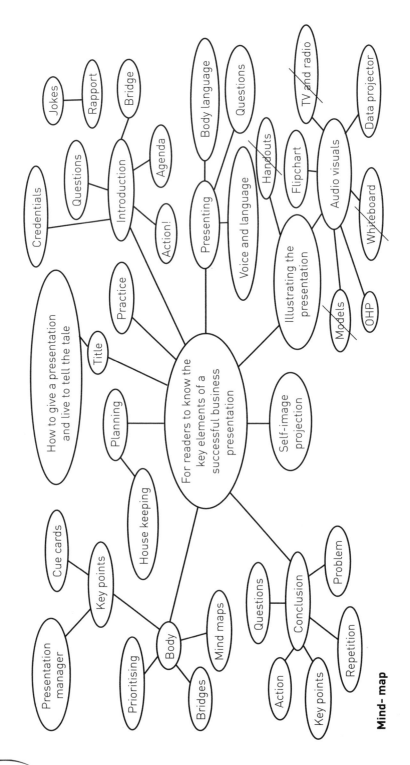

Mind- map

- To avoid sounding hackneyed, use a different bridge to move from each of your key points.

Now write them on your presentation planner.

Your introduction

You get one opportunity to make a first impression. So how do you create that positive impression from the start?

The first step is to establish empathy by building a bridge to as many audience members as you can. If you can, speak informally to each person before you begin.

When you stand to address the group, reinforce the bridge by saying how much you've been looking forward to meeting them . . . and pay some compliment to their office, factory, etc.

If you're considering starting with a joke, my advice is don't. You never know who you may offend and alienate. This isn't to say you shouldn't be warm, friendly and charming. But, as well as having the potential to offend, comedy is the most difficult of all stage techniques to master, as any actor will tell you.

Now say what you're going to talk about, as seen from their viewpoint. But why should they listen to you? You should say a few words here about why you are qualified to speak on this topic, what you have done to research the subject, what your background is in this field, etc. Two or three sentences can establish your credibility.

Now for the agenda. Give the audience a 'map' of what you'll be talking about. The agenda is a list of the key points which make up the body of the presentation. 'As we go through the presentation please feel free to ask questions, if I haven't explained anything clearly – although there will be a few moments at the end for questions.' Let's face it, telling people to save their questions until the end rarely works. So why not prepare for it? Doing it this way also signals to the audience that you're confident of what your talking about.

Next, state quite clearly what you want them to do as a result of listening to you – the action request. 'When I've finished speaking I hope you will see that the strategy I am advocating will help to re-position (product) in the marketplace.'

And finally your bridge. How do you link to the first key point in the body?

Now write each of these into your presentation planner.

The conclusion

Your conclusion should be short and to the point, but not rushed. You want to encapsulate your presentation into a package that they can take away with them.

Remind them of the problem or opportunity. Restate your key points and crystallise the message. State your request action – what you want them to do?

This structure for your presentation ensures that your key points are repeated at least three times and repetition is a very powerful persuader. Just watch commercial television to see how often advertisements are repeated if you need convincing.

Now write your conclusion on your presentation planner.

To summarise, with apologies to whoever said it first, your structure will allow you to 'Tell them what you're going to tell them, then tell them, and then tell them what you've told them.'

Plan your resources

Now you have decided what you are going to say, you can concentrate on how you say it. Transfer your introduction, key points (in the correct order) and conclusion on to postcards, using single words to act as stab points. Do not write a script, it will make your voice become dull and lifeless.

Now punch a hole in the top right-hand corner of each card and loosely tie them together with a piece of string. This will keep your presentation in the correct order, even if you drop the cards. When you deliver your presentation, don't be afraid to glance at your cue cards. A momentary pause is far more acceptable than waffle, or a deathly hush because you can't think what to say next.

Visual aids are useful in your presentation since they can convey information – try describing in words the layout of a printed circuit board or how to fold a napkin! Your visual aids reinforce what you are saying by focusing the audience's attention.

The most convenient visual aids to use are flipcharts or overhead transparencies. Both are available at good commercial stationers.

The flipchart can be very useful for developing diagrams in front of your audience – write the words/draw the diagram in advance lightly in pencil on the flipchart sheet. The audience will not be able to see the fine lines and you will be confident that the layout will be correct when you start to build up the chart in front of your audience using marker pens. Ensure that you have at least two pens available and check that they both work before the presentation.

Overhead transparencies are a convenient way of producing visual aids. Nowadays, you'll be out of the running, if you're applying for anything other than the most junior position, if you don't use one of the software packages like PowerPoint . You may even be asked to take your presentation visuals on a floppy disk or CD, so that they can be projected using an electronic data projector (see next section). If you don't have access to a computer, many high street print-shops can produce your transparencies for you. They can also photocopy diagrams or words directly onto transparencies. In an emergency and as an absolute last resort, you can use special pens to mark the transparencies up (I prefer the permanent kind since they do not smudge). Use only dark colours – pretty as the yellows and oranges are, they can't be read! That said, PowerPoint has become the standard for producing presentations so here are some tips.

Making your point with PowerPoint

If you've never used PowerPoint to create a presentation, ask around amongst your friends for some help. PowerPoint is a tremendous tool in helping to creating powerful presentations. With a few clicks of a mouse you can bring a car, a caribou or even Concorde into the room!

However, we've all heard the expression 'death by PowerPoint'. Too many people confuse the medium with the message, and use all the whistles and bells of PowerPoint to create boring repetitive screen shows or confusing circus acts, with fade-ins and -outs and all the other trickery!

Here are my top ten tips for getting the best out of PowerPoint.

- Use a consistent slide design with an uncluttered background for all your pages. Create a master page (Menu Bar/View/Master/Slide Master) and the layout will then be consistent for all the new pages you create.

- Use a consistent colour palette – don't start to fiddle around with the colours that are recommended in the font or text palette – they are there because they complement each other and don't clash.

- Avoid sending your audience to sleep by using page after page of bullet points and subheadings – words on a screen are not visual aids! Use short stab points like you see on a billboard. Don't put your script on the screen!

- Use visuals whenever you can! BUT avoid using the Microsoft clipart or sound files that came with your PC – they've seen it all before. Use your scanner, your digital camera, a clip art library from your computer store or trawl the Net. For example, if you right click on the company's logo on their website, you can save it to 'My pictures' and then use it in your presentation as an image in the footer, so that it's there on every slide.

- Include diagrams and flow charts – a picture is worth a thousand words! Better still a 10 to 15 second clip of video – but if you know how to add clips of video you probably don't need these tips!

- When you've created the presentation ask 'What can I edit out and still keep the meaning?' Be ruthless when editing – cut out everything that is not absolutely necessary. Work on the basis of about one slide for every minute of your presentation.

- Use only one font throughout. If you want to emphasise a word, use font size, bold, italic or colour, but don't underline.

- When people look at a new slide, their eyes will move from the top-left to the bottom-right of the screen. Artists quote the two-thirds/one-third rule for creating balance in a picture. In a nutshell, put your visual 'bottom-right' two-thirds down and one-third from the right.

- If you use transitions, use the same simple one throughout until you want to highlight a change of subject or really emphasise a point.

- Remember that each slide is part of a process. So when you've finished, run the slideshow to make sure that the sequence flows comfortably, and fits in with the 'story' which you developed using the Presentation Planner.

Remember if you emphasise *everything*, you emphasise nothing. KISS – keep it sweet and simple. On the logistical side of things, do what you can to make sure that you will be able to read your file in the software on their PC when you come to present it. If you've got the latest version of the software and they have an older version there may be problems. Why not save a couple of versions to CD just to be sure? When I give talks at conferences I usually e-mail a copy to the organiser, take a copy on CD and also take my laptop with a copy on the hard drive. You might think I'm a bit neurotic, but I've never had a problem. Unlike one friend of mine who picked up his ultraslim notebook and cracked the hard drive just before a presentation. Or another friend who tried to be clever by using an obscure font – unfortunately the font wasn't installed on the PC at the conference centre. They both 'busked' their way through, but I guess it's not really what you'd want to do at a job interview!

Whichever visual aids you use, follow the basic principle of keeping them as simple as possible. Use large letters and single words as stab points so that they can be read easily. Do not write complete sentences. Remember, a picture is worth a thousand words. As a general rule allow about one minute per transparency or slide when planning your time.

Practise

Rehearse your presentation once or twice so that you know what you are going to say and how you are going to say it. Use a friend as a timekeeper and to give you constructive feedback.

Answering questions

Generally speaking, assessors are aware of your time pressures and so will save their questions until the end. If you're asked a question that you can't answer then be honest – you'll gain more credibility from this than from half-baked waffle. You can in fact turn your lack of knowledge to your advantage by answering: 'That's an interesting point which I haven't been asked before. I'm afraid I don't have an answer for you right now but I will find out and get back to you.' This technique flatters the questioner's ego and demonstrates your integrity.

Preparation and presentation

Get a good night's sleep and no matter how nervous you are, avoid alcohol or stimulants!

Here are a few dos and don'ts for you to bear in mind when presenting.

Do	Don't
Use global vision to include everyone	Use non-words, like ums and errs
Hold eye contact with people	Jingle coins/keys in pockets
Check the power situation beforehand	Clean out/scratch orifices
Check the focus of the projector beforehand	Talk to the floor, the screen or one main audience member
Set up the room beforehand	Read visuals word for word
Use clear, concise visuals	Joke – you don't know who you might offend
Vary the tone and speed of your voice	Mumble
Stand relatively still	Apologise for what you're going to say
Have spare pens/transparencies	Dress outrageously
Keep to time	Smoke – even if some audience members do
Use simple language	Remove your jacket
End on a positive note	Use a pointer – they're too easy to play with

What are the assessors looking for ?

Unless you've applied for a job as a television presenter or a similar position which involves speaking to groups on a regular basis, it is unlikely that the assessors will be looking for outstanding skills.

The assessors will be looking for you to communicate your message effectively, for you to project yourself confidently and for you to know what you are talking about. They'll also be trying to gauge how much work you have put into the exercise and how seriously you took it. I once ran an assessment centre in which two of the candidates were 'late entries'. Each received the briefing pack only the day before. One candidate gave a very poor talk from some scribbled notes and apologised, making the excuse that she hadn't had time to prepare. The other candidate gave an excellent presentation, with professionally produced transparencies, and handouts of her talk for the assessors. She made no mention of the short amount of time she'd had to prepare. Let me ask, who do you think made the best impression? And, everything else being equal, who would you have employed?

Finally, remember that even the most experienced presenters get nervous – use the adrenalin to help you to excel!

There follows an example of a form that may be used to assess your presentation. It is accompanied by a suggested format which may be useful when planning a presentation.

Assessment Centre – Presentation Score Sheet

Candidate name: _____   Assessor: _____

Ten-minute presentation with five minutes of questions and answers from assessors.

Criteria	Comments	Rating
Content		
Delivery (voice/posture)		
Pace		
Use of visuals		
Audience contact		
Handling questions		
Other comments		

Standards

5   Much more than acceptable (significantly above the criteria required for successful job performance)

4   More than acceptable (generally exceeds the criteria relative to quality and quantity of behaviour required)

3   Acceptable (meets the criteria relative to quality and quantity of behaviour required)

2   Less than acceptable (generally does not meet the criteria relative to quality and quantity of behaviour required)

1   Much less than acceptable (significantly below the criteria required for successful job performance)

Overall rating _____

Presentation planner

Introduction	Main body	Conclusion
Rapport statement	Key point 1	Remind them of the problem/opportunity
Presentation subject	Bridge	
Your credentials	Key point 2	Restate the key points and crystallise the message
Agenda	Bridge	
Question request	Key point 3	
	Bridge	
Action request	Key point 4	Request action
	Bridge	
Bridge	Key point 5	
	Bridge	

CHAPTER THIRTY-FOUR

Recruitment tests and evaluations

Personality, skill and aptitude evaluations

'It is hard to fail, but it is worse never to have tried to succeed. In this life we get nothing save by effort.'

Theodore Roosevelt

Some organisations use tests and evaluations in their selection process. Before inviting people to interview, the recruiter identifies personality traits, skills and knowledge which the ideal candidate would have. During the selection process candidates are asked to complete 'tests' to evaluate whether they possess these qualities.

The extent of the testing can vary from a short five-minute form-filling exercise through to a whole day, involving a battery of tests and evaluations and an interview with a psychologist.

I cannot stress too strongly that there is no need to get anxious about the tests! I know it's easy for me to say that . . . I'm not the one who has been invited to interview! Seriously, the tests will not reveal that really you are an alien from Mars (you aren't, are you?) or that you're not really a person but a slug that lives in an aquarium and just for today you've transformed yourself into a person! Take them in your stride, do your best and be honest.

You should also read the *Test Taker's Guide* article which is presented later in this chapter. This has been contributed by ASE, one of the leading providers of psychometric assessment and consulting services in the UK and so their advice is well worth taking!

Personality questionnaires

As the name implies, these questionnaires aim to gain an insight into your personality. I do not like the use of the word 'test' when related to personality evaluations. 'Test' implies 'right or wrong' and in personality evaluations there are no right and wrong answers – we are all different.

Usually no time limit is set for completing a personality questionnaire, but you are advised not to over-analyse your replies and to move quickly from question to question. Don't answer questions as you think you *should*. Be honest to yourself, otherwise you're defeating the object. Also, some personality questionnaires have an in-built evaluation which checks to see how consistent (honest) your answers have been.

The most commonly used personality questionnaires are:

- the Myers-Briggs Type Inventory (MBTI), which claims to be the most widely used in the world
- the SHL Occupational Personality Quotient (SHL OPQ)
- the Sixteen Personality Factors (16PF)
- and one by Thomas International.

There are many others.

Skill and aptitude tests

Unlike personality questionnaires, skill and aptitude tests *are* designed to test you against standards.

Typing tests are used to evaluate your keyboard skills and typing accuracy. Tests of manual dexterity, such as rebuilding a broken-down model, assess your 'motor skills'.

Others represent an intellectual challenge – numerical, verbal and abstract reasoning tests are described under the *Test Taker's Guide* and in the section about psychometric testing later in this chapter.

The score from the tests is compared against 'norm' tables to see how you have performed, compared with previous groups of people who have taken the test.

On the following pages is a *Test Taker's Guide*. The 'general ability tests' are used for the selection of staff below graduate level and for the identification of potential for supervisory and junior management posts, regardless of previous experience or education. The 'graduate and managerial assessment' tests are used in recruiting at graduate and managerial level.

I am grateful to ASE for their permission to reproduce this guide.

GENERAL ABILITY TESTS
A TEST TAKER'S GUIDE

- You have been sent this leaflet to help you prepare for your testing session. It:
- Introduces you to the tests themselves;
- gives you an idea of what to expect;
- provides hints on how to prepare yourself;
- answers key questions – but remember that you can still ask questions at the testing session

Here are the answers to some important questions.

Q Why am I being asked to take some tests?

A   You may have school or work qualifications, but these tests give extra information which will help employers to select those applicants who are best suited to the job or their training programme.

Tests also help you to explore your abilities; this should assist you in choosing a suitable area of work.

People who are successful in the job have usually done well in the tests, so both employers and applicants get what they want.

Q How do they work?

A   Employers decide which skills and abilities are needed in the job. Tests are then selected to measure some of these.

There is a practice period in the testing session to make sure everyone understands how to do the test(s).

The tests are carefully timed, so you may not finish; but you should work as fast as you can and follow the instructions given.

Your answers are then scored and this information is used to help decide whether you will be suitable for the job.

Q Will I be asked to do anything else?

A   Usually you will be asked to fill in an application form and this information is also very important.

You may also be interviewed. Employers use information from many sources to help them make the best decision.

THE TEST SESSION
When you come to the session you will be asked to do the tests ticked below. The time shown beside each test is the time you will be allowed once you have read the introductory examples and done the practice test. Remember, you will be given a break between the tests.

—————	Verbal	15 minutes
—————	Numerical	20 minutes
—————	Non-verbal	20 minutes
—————	Spatial	20 minutes

Look at the examples given for each of the tests you will be taking. None of these examples will be in the real tests.

Check that you understand the questions and correct answers. Remember that if you do not understand there will be time to ask before the test begins.

THE ANSWER SHEET

You will be given a separate answer sheet for each test. The one given below is from the Verbal Test and is marked with the correct answers for the examples given. The Numerical and Non-Verbal answer sheets are very similar.

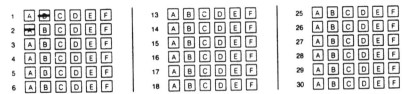

Below is a section from the Spatial answer sheet. The correct answers to Examples 1 to 4 are marked.

VERBAL

This test is about relationships between pairs of words. In each question you are given one pair of words and you have to find out how they are related. Then you have to choose a word, from the six given, which would complete another pair of words. The missing word is shown by a question mark. The second pair must be related to each other in the same way as the pair you have been given.

In the two examples below the correct answers are highlighted: 'clothes' is the answer to Example 1, and 'line' is the answer to Example 2.

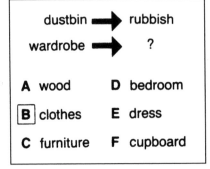

Example 1

Example 2

NON-VERBAL

In this test you have to work out relationships between shapes. There are two basic types of question. In the first, as Example 1, you are given two large figures inside an oval. You have to decide how they are alike, which may be in one way or several ways. Only one figure at the bottom also has all these qualities. In this case there is a small shape followed by a dotted line, then two solid lines. Only figure A fits this description. The correct answer has been highlighted.

In the other questions, such as Examples 2 and 3, there is a grid which contains an arrangement of shapes with

one missing section. This is marked by the question mark. You have to decide how the shapes are related to each other and decide which of the six possibilities is the missing one.

In Example 2, the three figures in the centre of each big triangle are repeated in the outer triangles next to them. Also, each repeated figure has either a circle or a triangle around it. Here, the answer is 'F'.

In Example 3, a different grid is used. The answer, which is 'A', can be found by looking at the pattern of shapes in the inside and outside triangles.

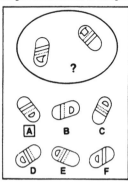

Example 1

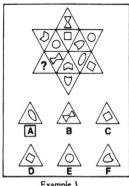

Example 2

Example 3

NUMERICAL

In this test you have to work out the relationship between numbers. All questions have an arrangement of numbers in a grid with one or two numbers missing. The missing numbers are shown by question marks. You have to find how the numbers are related to each other and so decide which of the six possibilities is the missing one.

If you look at the first example below, the numbers in the 'chain' on the left-hand side go in sequence by 'doubling up'. Thus, twice 3 is 6; twice 6 is 12; and twice 12 is 24. Therefore the missing answer is 24 or 'C'. The correct answer has been highlighted.

Sometimes you have two numbers missing and you will have to find the answer which has them both. In Example 2 you have to look across the rows and down the columns rather like a crossword. Going across the rows, the numbers increase by the same amount; going down the rows they double each time. You must find the two numbers that fit both of these rules. The missing numbers are 14 and 20, which is answer 'A'.

In Example 3, you again must find the two missing numbers. Here, the bottom number on the left is always 21 more than the top number, and the one on the right is always 10 more than the top numbers. Thus, the correct answer is 'A'.

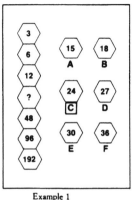

Example 1

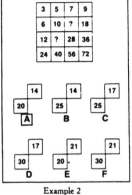

Example 2

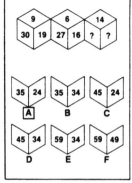

Example 3

SPATIAL

In this test you have to imagine what a flat pattern would look like if it were cut out and folded into a solid object. The patterns have to be folded along the black lines so that the markings are on the outside of the solid object.

You have to decide if each of the solid objects shown below the flat pattern could be made from it when folded. Answer 'no' if an object definitely **could not** be made and 'yes' if it definitely **could** be made. If you cannot be sure without seeing the hidden side, answer 'yes'.

In Example 1, if the pattern were folded it would form a long shape with one black side and the dot in the middle on one of the ends. Question 1 clearly could be this shape with the black side and dot in the correct places. Similarly, the answer to question 2 is 'yes' since there is one black side and you can only see one of the ends; the other one could have the dot on it. However, the answer to question 3 is clearly 'no' since the long side on the top left should be black. Question 4 is 'yes' because the black side is hidden under the shape. The correct answers are under the questions.

In Example 2 the answers to questions 5, 6 and 7 are 'yes', while the answer to 8 is 'no'.

Example 1

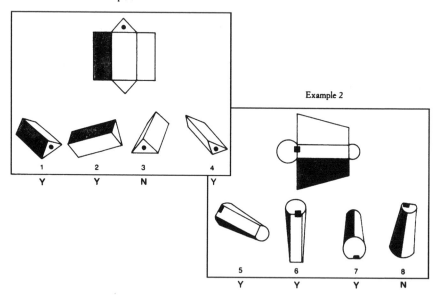

Example 2

Q How can I prepare myself for the test?

● Prepare yourself by having a good night's sleep and arriving well in time.

● If you normally wear glasses or a hearing aid remember to bring them with you.

● Read this leaflet carefully and make sure you understand what to expect from the tests you will be doing.

Q How do I do my best in the tests?

● Don't be afraid to ask a question if there is something not clear to you.

● Listen carefully and follow the instructions given as well as you can.

● Remember that most tests are timed, so work quickly and accurately without wasting time on those questions you do not understand.

● If it is a long time since you did an exam or test, do not worry! Test results, if used correctly, should give a fair assessment regardless of your age, race, sex or background.

Published by the NFER-NELSON Publishing Company Ltd, Darville House, 2 Oxford Road East, Windsor, Berkshire SL4 1DF.
Printed in Great Britain.   2(4.90)   Code 4025 10 4

GRADUATE AND MANAGERIAL ASSESSMENT

A Test Taker's Guide

Part of our organisation's selection system involves the use of tests. The reason for using tests is simply to collect as much information as possible about each person to help us make a more informed and fairer decision.

You have been sent this leaflet to help you prepare for your testing session. It has been designed to:

- introduce you to the tests themselves;
- give you an idea of what to expect;
- provide hints on how to prepare yourself;
- answer key questions – but remember that you can still ask questions at the testing session.

Here are the answers to some important questions.

Q Why am I being asked to take some tests?

A You may have work, training or vocational qualifications, but these tests give extra information which will help us to select people who are best suited to the job or who will benefit from a development or training programme. People who are successful in the job tend to do well in the tests, so everybody gets what they want.

Q How do they work?

A We have found out which skills and abilities are needed in the job. We then chose tests to measure some of these skills and abilities.

There is a practice period in each test to make sure everyone understands how to do it. Remember you can ask questions during the practice period. The tests are carefully timed, and you probably will not finish; but remember to work as fast as you can and to follow the instructions given. Do not spend too long on any one question. Toward the end of each test, review your answers and the questions you have not answered. At this stage, even if you are not absolutely sure of an answer, make it anyway. There is no penalty for guessing and any answer is better than none at all.

When the test is over your answers will be scored and this information will be used to help decide whether you will be suitable for the job or training programme.

Q Will I be asked to do anything else?

A You may be interviewed or asked to take part in practical exercises or group activities. We use information from as many sources as possible to help us make the best decision.

The Test Session

When you come to the session you will be asked to do one or more of the tests ticked below. The time shown beside each test is the time you will be allowed after you have been given the introductory examples and practice test. Remember you will be given a break between the tests.

☐	Abstract	30 minutes
☐	Verbal	30 minutes
☐	Numerical	30 minutes

·Look at the examples overleaf for each of the tests you will be taking. None of these examples will be in the real tests. Check that you understand the questions and correct answers. Reading them more than once may help you understand them. Remember that if you have questions there will be time to ask before the test begins.

The Answer Sheet

You will be given a separate answer sheet for each test. Here is part of the abstract answer sheet. It is marked with the correct answers for the examples given below. The Verbal and Numerical answer sheets are very similar.

```
 1  ⬤  IB  IC
 2  IA  ⬤  IC
 3  IA'  IB'  ⬤
 4  IA'  IB  ⬤
 5  ⬤  IB  IC
 
 6  IA'  IB!  ICI
 7  IAi  IB!  ICI
 8  IA'  IB  IC'
 9  IA'  IB  IC'
10  IA  IB  IC
```

Abstract

This is a test of your skill at finding similarities and differences in groups of patterns. Each item consists of three sets of patterns. There are two groups of four, one marked A and another marked B, and a set of five separate patterns which are numbered.

All the patterns in Group A are in some way similar to each other, and all those in Group B are similar to each other. However, the two groups are different, and you should be able to identify the basis for this difference by studying them.

When you have worked out why the patterns in Groups A and B are grouped as they are, you should then decide to which group each of the five separately numbered patterns belongs.

If you decide that a pattern belongs to Group A, put a line through A next to that pattern's number on the answer sheet. Similarly, if you decide that a pattern belongs to Group B, put a line through B. If you decide that a pattern belongs to neither Group A nor Group B then put a line through C on the answer sheet.

Incidentally, the patterns in the A and B groups are in no particular arrangement or order, so don't waste time looking for sequences amongst the groups of four, or matches between patterns in the A and B Groups in corresponding positions.

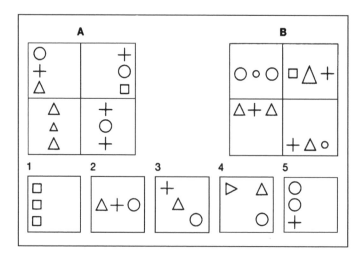

In the example above, each pattern in Group A consists of shapes arranged vertically; and each of the Group B patterns consist of shapes arranged horizontally. So patterns 1 and 5 belong with Group A, pattern 2 belongs with Group B and patterns 3 and 4 do not belong to either, so they are in Group C.

Verbal

This is a test of your skill at making sense of reports which cannot be relied upon to be objective, truthful or even consistent.

The test consists of a series of short passages of prose, each of which includes a number of statements intended to convey information, or persuade the reader of a point of view.

Each passage is accompanied by four statements relating to the information or arguments it contains. Assume that what is stated in the passage is true – even if it contradicts what you know or believe to be the case in reality – and decide for each statement whether, on this assumption, it is true or false, or whether you cannot tell and need more information.

The definitions are:

True: This means that the statement is already made in the passage, that it is implied by, or follows logically from a statement or statements made in the passage.

False: This means that the statement contradicts a statement made in, implied by, or following logically from, the passage.

Can't tell: This means that there is insufficient information in the passage to draw firm conclusions about the truth or falsity of the statement.

In recent years it has become clear that man's use of fossil fuels is likely to have a major impact on the world's climate. As a result of this, increased concentrations of 'greenhouse' gases such as carbon dioxide and methane will lead to global warming – an overall small increase in average temperatures – whose impact is difficult to predict. Whilst some scientists predict melting of the polar icecaps, and so a rise in sea levels, others think this will be balanced by increased precipitation at the poles.

---

1 If we go on using fossil fuels at the present rate, we must expect climatic change.

2 Depletion of the ozone layer will result in global warming.

3 Scientists are agreed that use of fossil fuels will eventually lead to a rise in sea levels.

4 The burning of fossil fuels increases the concentration of methane in the atmosphere.

A True   **B False**   **C Can't tell**

In the example above, the answers to 1 and 4 are 'A'. The statements are true on the basis of the information given in the first two sentences of the passage. The answer to 2 is 'C'. No information about the ozone layer is given in the passage so it is impossible to tell whether the statement is true or false. The answer to 3 is 'B'. The statement is false because it contradicts the information given in the last sentence of the passage.

Numerical

This is a test of your skill at reasoning with numbers. First, you are given some information in a variety of forms – text, tables or graphs – followed by three related questions. For each question, choose what you think is the correct answer from the possible answers A to P.

An insurance scheme pays benefits to its members who are sick for extended periods of time at the following rates:

1st month:	*nil*
2nd – 4th months:	*50% of normal salary*
5th and succeeding months:	*25% of normal salary*

on the first £24,000 p.a. of salary for each month in which the member is sick and is not paid by the employer.
How much does the scheme pay to:

1 | John, who is off work for two months, whose salary is £12,000 p.a., and who gets no sick pay.

2 | Pat, who is ill for 6 months, but who is paid normally for the first two months and whose salary is £18,000 p.a..

3 | Hilary, whose salary is £30,000 p.a., who gets 3 months' sick pay from her employer, and who has to take 9 months off.

A	£250	B	£500	C	£750	D	£1000
E	£1125	F	£1500	G	£1765	H	£2125
I	£2250	J	£2350	K	£2500	L	£3125
M	£3750	N	£4000	O	£5000	P	£5625

In the example above the answer to 1 is 'B'. The answer to 2 is 'I'. The answer to 3 is 'N'. Remember that, in this example, the scheme operates 'for each month in which the member is sick and is not paid by the employer'. So the scheme only comes into effect once the employer's sick pay stops. Careful reading of the information given will help you answer the questions correctly.

Q   How can I prepare myself for the tests?

- Prepare yourself by having a good night's sleep and arriving well in time.
- If you normally wear glasses or a hearing aid remember to bring them with you.
- Read this leaflet carefully and make sure you understand what to expect from the tests you will be doing.

Q   How do I do my best in the tests?

- Don't be afraid to ask a question if there is something not clear to you.
- Listen carefully and follow the instructions given as well as you can.
- Remember that most tests are timed, so try to work quickly and accurately.
- If it is a long time since you did an exam or test, do not worry! Test results, if used correctly, should give a fair assessment regardless of your age, race, sex or background.

a s e

Published by The NFER–NELSON Publishing Company Ltd., Darville House,
2 Oxford Road East. Windsor, Berkshire, SL4 1DF, England.
© 1992, S.F. Blinkhorn
All rights reserved.
Code 4700 14 4

Team type questionnaires

Work by Dr Meredith Belbin has shown that groups are most productive when there is a good mixture of people who can contribute various skills to the team. The organisation will analyse the members of the existing team The 'team type' questionnaire is then used and your results are analysed manually or by software to see how you fit in.

None of the team types is the 'best' type to be – productive teams have a mix of the different types. The following summary describes the various team types.

- **Plant** – creative, imaginative, unorthodox. Solves difficult problems. Weak in communicating with and managing ordinary people.

- **Resource investigator** – extrovert, enthusiastic, communicative. Explores opportunities. Develops contacts. Loses interest once initial enthusiasm has passed.

- **Chairperson/coordinator** – mature, confident and trusting. A good chairperson clarifies goals, promotes decision-making. Not necessarily the most clever or creative member of a group.

- **Shaper** – dynamic, outgoing, highly strung. Challenges, pressurises, finds ways round obstacles. Prone to provocation and short-lived bursts of temper.

- **Monitor evaluator** – sober, strategic and discerning. Sees all options. Judges accurately. Lacks drive and ability to inspire others.

- **Teamworker** – social, mild, perceptive and accommodating. Listens, builds, averts friction. Indecisive in crunch situations.

- **Company worker/implementer** – disciplined, reliable, conservative and efficient. Turns ideas into practical actions. Somewhat inflexible, slow to respond to new possibilities.

- **Completer** – painstaking, conscientious, anxious. Searches out errors and omissions. Delivers on time. Inclined to worry unduly. Reluctant to delegate.

- **Expert/specialist** – single-minded, self-starting, dedicated. Provides knowledge or technical skills in rare supply. Contributes only on a narrow front.

To find out your own 'team type' you'll need Dr Meredith Belbin's book, *Management Teams: Why They Succeed or Fail*, which contains the questionnaire, and also a free voucher to take an online evaluation. You can also get useful information from *www.belbin.com*

Drug and alcohol testing

Because of their concern about the effect that alcohol and drug abuse has on productivity, some employers may require you to provide a urine sample which will be tested for drugs and alcohol. These tests are still quite rare in the UK but are common in the USA, so they are probably more likely to be encountered if you are applying to the UK affiliate of a large US company. Of course you can always refuse – but if you do so then you'll almost certainly eliminate yourself. I'm not here to debate the pros and cons, but common sense would suggest that if it's likely that you'll be tested and you're likely to test positive, then give yourself a clear period to 'detoxify' before the interview or medical check!

Graphology (handwriting analysis)

You won't even be aware that it's being carried out! Graphologists claim to be able to interpret the personality of a person from their handwriting. I understand that it is widely used in continental Europe, particularly in France and Germany, but not in the UK, although one UK consultancy offering this service has over 100 clients.

If you want to read more about drug and alcohol testing or graphology visit the website of the Chartered Institute of Personnel and Development, and use their search engine at *www.cipd.co.uk*.

Feedback

To end on a positive note, a good employer will always give you feedback from these tests, whether you get offered the job or not – but usually only if you ask!

Profiling instruments, evaluations, assessments, or whatever you wish to call them, are not free – they cost the recruiting organisation both time and money. If they're being used, they're serious about your application.

They are yet another way for you to show you're the right person for the job!

I am extremely grateful to Robert Edenborough, Managing Consultant of ASE, for the following contribution on psychometric testing.

Psychometric testing

E V O L U T I O N   @   W O R K

In applying for a job you are likely to be asked to sit a psychometric test or tests. 'Psychometric' simply means mental measurement and many of the tests are designed to 'measure' mental abilities.

Ability tests

Ability tests come in a number of forms and the examples shown earlier (the *Test Taker's Guide*, p.253) illustrate some of these. Common types are:

- numerical reasoning
- verbal reasoning
- spatial or mechanical reasoning
- abstract reasoning.

Numerical reasoning tests sometimes pose arithmetical problems of a type familiar from early school days. In other cases, the items require a degree of interpretation and understanding of the type of material being presented, as well as calculation. The second type seeks to reproduce some of the situations that people may come across in organisations, such as reading charts showing business trends. Usually a high level of mathematical expertise is not needed. The demands of doing the test come largely because they have to be completed within a time limit.

Verbal reasoning tests are also of two broad types. Some set tasks like the completion of sentences or the recognition of synonyms. At more advanced levels the format typically involves a passage of prose and a series of statements related to it. The statements have to be judged in terms of whether they reflect information in the passage.

Spatial tests may involve the identification of shapes that might have been rotated or three-dimensional figures to be unfolded. These problems are, however, commonly presented in two-dimensional booklet form. They are used in connection with jobs that require spatial reasoning of some sort which could range from working with engineering design drawings to planning the layout of a store.

Abstract tests are used to assess general reasoning ability. They may be of particular value if candidates are required to deal with entirely new ideas and concepts. They pose problems such as the identification of sequences in abstract patterns.

Personality

Most personality measures used are of the self-report questionnaire type. Sometimes they ask you to rate how far a particular statement applies to you. In other cases you are asked to choose which of a series of statements is most and which least like you. There is some debate as to whether these should be called 'tests' on the grounds that your personality is what it is and to refer to it in terms of testing is to imply that something is potentially *wrong* with the essence of who you are. Nevertheless, different personalities will fit differently well with different types of job and so in practice when personality measures are used in selection situations there is no doubt that you are being tested. However, the point often made in the introduction to personality questionnaires that there are 'no right or wrong answers' to individual questions is true in the sense that you are not being asked to solve problems but to indicate something about yourself and your typical behaviour.

You may wonder if it is possible to 'cheat' at personality tests. The first response to this must be why would you choose to do so? Do you feel that you should be other than you are? If you did 'cheat' and got a job as a result you would be unlikely to be comfortable in the job and probably would not cope. Thus if you thought that some items in a test were to do with orderliness, even though you yourself are rather slapdash in your approach to things, and you chose all the statements that described you as orderly you would probably not have the systematic approach needed for the job. You would feel bored, you would probably miss the detail and would be unlikely to last very long. Also it is quite likely that you would not get as far as being offered a job – for many personality measures there are built in checks that give an indication that distortion is occurring.

Use and interpretation of tests

An employer will be using ability measures and personality questionnaires to find out broadly how someone will cope with the particular intellectual demands of a job on the one hand, and how they will conduct themselves in approaching tasks, interacting with others and perhaps dealing with pressure on the other. In order to make these interpretations your performance will usually be compared with that of a 'norm group' of others. Because of this, just how difficult an ability test seemed to be as you went through it may not be much of a guide as to how you have done – the interpretation of your performance depends on comparing it with the standard set by the norm group.

Those working with tests and personality questionnaires should abide by the professional standards laid down by the British Psychological Society and the Institute of Personnel and Development. Among other things, these say that feedback should be given to those tested. If this is not forthcoming when you are tested, ask about it! For personality measures, feedback is often used as part of a further discussion with you as the candidate. This is partly to check that the measure is giving a realistic picture of you. It is also to provide further information to expand the indications from the questionnaire. To stick with the example of orderliness, if you appear to be high on this you may be asked to give evidence of situations where you have demonstrated this and where it has been particularly important in the past.

Sometimes ability tests will be used as part of a screening process, and sometimes to provide additional information on a group of candidates all of whom have been shortlisted. In the screening case a definite cut-off score is likely to be applied. Where tests and questionnaires are used at the shortlist stage they may often result in a detailed report. This will be considered by a final selection panel along with other information such as that taken from a CV or from a presentation to the panel. Professional use of tests also requires that they should never be used as the sole determinant of whether or not someone is offered a job but should be set in the context of such other information.

Preparing for testing

The advice given for exams of 'get a good night's sleep' applies to testing. It is also a good idea to allow yourself plenty of time to arrive at the testing location and as far as possible to clear your mind of other matters. If you are waiting for the test to finish so that you can dash out and check for messages on your mobile phone you are unlikely to be giving the test your best shot!

There is also the question of what preparation can be made by practice in advance. The guidance here is to familiarise yourself with the type of material available but not to over-practise which could lead to some distortion. There are a number of effective publications on the market to aid familiarity. Also, you will quite often be sent information by an employer to help you prepare for specific tests, such as those illustrated earlier in this chapter.

Tests and career guidance

You may, of course, take an initiative and put yourself through some tests in order to find out about your capacities and inclinations. A number of bodies offer services of this type. In addition to the ability and personality measures described here, you may be asked to complete a motivational questionnaire to suggest what your drives and satisfactions are or construct an interest inventory. These ask you to rate different elements of work and so build up a picture of the type of job that could interest you.

You may find the following useful.

- *Prepare for Tests at Interview for Graduates and Managers*, Robert Williams, London: ASE.

- *How to Pass Selection Tests*, Mike Bryon and Sanjay Modha, London: Kogan Page.

CHAPTER THIRTY-FIVE

What if you don't get the job you want

Learning from experience

'Every noble work is at first impossible.'

Thomas Carlyle

You made it to a shortlist of two. People were making such positive noises about how you would fit into the organisation. And then a letter this morning '. . . Thank you for attending interview . . . I am sorry to inform you that . . .' and the world falls away from under your feet.

Can you turn the situation to advantage ?

- Write to them quickly to say how disappointed you are and how impressed you had been with their company. Say that if any other vacancies arise in the near future you would like to be considered. Alternatively, telephone them to say the same things and to ask for some feedback on why you didn't get the job – most employers will give you some constructive critique and you never know, you may be able to re-open discussions – it can work. (See Chapter 28.)

- Follow up your letter with a phone call.

- What have you learned from the process? It may be not to put all your eggs in one basket or to conduct yourself differently at recruitment interviews.

CHAPTER THIRTY-SIX

What if you DO get offered the job you want?

Negotiating the best package

'Experience shows us that success is due less to ability than to zeal. The winner is the one who gives themselves to their work; body and soul.'

Charles Buxton

Congratulate yourself! CELEBRATE!

And don't forget to say thank you to those who helped you on your way.

'Yippee, I got the new job!' (candidate's view). 'Yippee, I've filled the vacancy!' (employer's view). It's what's called a win–win scenario by negotiators. Both parties have benefited.

As soon as your potential employer starts to display buying signals you should be ready to begin the negotiation concerning your earnings package.

I've said earlier that you should let the employer raise the issue of salary first, but you should also realise that they may not necessarily make their best offer up-front.

'Yippee – I've filled the vacancy!' 'Yippee – I got the job'

Negotiating the best package

'What we obtain too cheap, we esteem too lightly; it is dearness only that gives everything its value.'

Thomas Paine

In some occupations, salaries are fixed according to seniority and length of service. In others there is a good deal of flexibility around certain variables. Remember, when you have accepted an offer, you have accepted it. You'll create a bad impression if you accept the job and then go back two days later, trying to renegotiate the terms of the contract.

So before you enter the negotiating arena it's worth working out the minimum package you are prepared to accept and what you would like to get. Realistically, there will be some aspects of the package which will be fixed, for example holidays, and which will be written in policies and procedures.

Knowledge is power

The table at the end of this chapter is taken from a real salary survey (kindly supplied by Alan Jones Associates) with the job title removed for confidentiality. Salary surveys are produced by agencies that gather (confidential) information from many organisations on the salaries paid to people at all levels (but names are never released). This information is 'pooled' and analysed, and then shared between the contributing organisations. HR managers can then look at the tables to see how their organisation's salaries compare with others, and use the data when preparing job offers. Salary surveys can be specific to a particular industry or profession, or they can be based geographically.

Some organisations, which 'want to recruit the best' have a philosophy of paying at the 'ninetieth percentile' – they pay better than 90 per cent of their competitors. Others pay at the median – halfway up the scale. But remember that for every high payer there's another at the bottom of the scale!

This 'range' is illustrated in the example I have shown. The absolute numbers are irrelevant, but the range is very important. As you can see, there are large differences between the minimum and maximum salaries and values of company cars. The lowest paid job pays £17,000 a year with no company car, while the highest pays almost £32,000 with a £15,000 company car. A huge difference, yet these people hold the same job title but in different organisations. If everything else was equal, which job would you prefer?

While you are in the discussing phase of negotiation, before anything is committed to paper, ask:

- Where does the salary fit into their internal salary scales?
- Where does the salary fit in the salary surveys, for a person with similar experience doing a similar job?

Company policy may be that they pay a 'lower quartile' salary (in other words 75 per cent of people doing a similar job earn more) to a new starter, with the objective of shifting you to the upper quartile within three years. Try to convince them that your skills and experience warrant being started higher up the scale.

Don't be greedy, but do be thorough. Many of the employment agency websites contain salary calculators and advice. Also remember that you probably won't be able to renegotiate a package once you have accepted it so tread carefully. An extra £500 per year over a career is an awful lot of money!

JOB 88: CONFIDENTIAL

TOTAL NUMBER OF JOBHOLDERS : 70
NO. OF COMPANIES REPORTING : 19

COMPANY CODE(L)	JOB HLDRS	MOD MNTH	RATE MNTH	SALARY RANGE MINIMUM	SALARY RANGE CONTROL	SALARY RANGE MAXIMUM	ACTUAL AVERAGE BASIC	BonusV	BonusF	TOTAL	COMPA RATIO	ACTUAL MEDIAN BASIC	BonusV	BonusF	TOTAL	COMPA RATIO	CAR VALUE
01	1	=	5	25142	31428	37713	31250	0	601	31851	99	31250	0	601	31851	99	15184
28	2	=	17	29425	26574	33900	23261	4280	447	27988	88	23261	4280	447	27988	88	13655
03	1	=	11	24549	30066	36814	26586	0	1108	27694	88	26586	0	1108	27694	88	17050
10	1	=	7	23606	29508	35410	26000	0	0	26000	88	26000	0	0	26000	88	14000
18	8	=	11	19945	24170	29385	23599	1244	0	25316	81	23100	1200	0	24420	95	13500
22	2	=	1	23300	29124	34949	24802	726	991	24882	101	24365	726	991	24365	97	13000
07	4	=	3	20182	25227	30272	23400	808	662	24470	100	23100	808	662	24470	100	17040
19	1	=	1	22300	23100	33440	23400	880	0	24320	84	23238	347	0	23585	88	15300
02	6	=	8	19731	27870	29596	21704	1953	0	23657	88	21704	1953	0	23857	88	11500
16	2	=	11	21122	24664	31785	21753	1750	0	23513	82	22200	1845	0	23865	89	14354
17	4	=	1	20097	26454	30146	22723	0	0	22723	90	22250	0	0	22250	93	13634
11	12	=	1	19588	25122	26342	19902	567	1558	21627	93	19502	567	1558	21460	93	
24	1	=	1	17562	20859	25030	21150	810	0	21460	94	20650	810	0	21250	98	15000
14	3	=	10	17379	21724	26069	19875	0	0	21250	98	21250	0	0	21250	94	
29	4	=	1	18000	19875	26069	18900	0	0	19875	100	19875	0	0	19875	98	12700
05	4	=	8	18640	22840	27035	18633	900	0	19820	83	19125	695	0	19820	84	
20	7	=	7	18300	19900	21500	18633	0	0	18633	94	18300	0	0	18300	92	11389
12	3	=	0	12819	14594	16282	17000	0	0	17000	116	17000	0	0	17000	116	

	SALARY RANGE ++CONTROL++ UNWTD	WTD	ACTUAL AVERAGE ++BASIC++ UNWTD	WTD	++TOTAL++ UNWTD	WTD	ACTUAL MEDIAN ++BASIC++ UNWTD	WTD	++TOTAL++ UNWTD	WTD	CAR VALUE UNWTD
MAXIMUM	31428	31428	31250	31250	31851	31851	31250	31250	31851	31851	17050
UPPER QUARTILE	27222	25227	24037	23440	25517	24882	23075	23075	24943	24200	15138
MEDIAN	24664	24417	22713	22713	22713	22713	22250	22250	23657	22250	13827
AVERAGE	24476	23947	21974	21974	23572	23572	21687	21687	23403	22379	14093
LOWER QUARTILE	21838	21952	20262	19875	21355	19875	20262	19875	21355	19875	13125
MINIMUM	14594	14594	17000	17000	17000	17000	17000	17000	17000	17000	11389

CHAPTER THIRTY-SEVEN

Saying goodbye to your employer

Departing diplomatically

'Don't flatter yourself that friendship authorises you to say disagreeable things to your intimates. The nearer you come into relation with a person, the more necessary do tact and courtesy become.'

Oliver Wendell Holmes

The practical aspects

Make sure you know the name of the pension fund administrator so that you can keep them updated of changes of address and whether you want to change pension schemes.

The personal aspects

If you are leaving on bad terms DON'T, DON'T, DON'T be rude, abusive or disrespectful to your ex-employer. No matter how much venom there is on the inside, control it and keep it there.

Now, I'm not offering this advice in the interests of your ex-employers, but in yours. No matter how bitter you are feeling, try to leave on amicable terms. The reason for this is that most new employers will want a reference from your past employer. Even if you don't need it immediately for a new job, you might need it in a year or two.

You'll do neither your self-esteem nor your future job prospects any good if you lose your temper and are abusive to your boss. If you want to vent your anger try writing a letter to your ex-boss. Don't hold anything back. When you've finished, and said everything you want to say, tear it up and throw it in the waste bin! It does work!!! (and if you've written it on a PC make sure it hasn't been saved!)

Try to 'negotiate' the wording of your reference before you leave so that it can be placed on your personnel file. People move on and it may be that, even only a few months after you have left an organisation, a personnel officer you have never met will complete a company reference for you and this will be based on the contents of your personnel file.

You can find tips and templates for writing your letter of resignation at *www.i-resign.com.*

CHAPTER THIRTY-EIGHT

Starting and keeping your new job

New kid on the block

'Ah, but a man's reach should exceed his grasp, Or what's heaven for?'

Robert Browning

Congratulations! What you have reached for has come within your grasp! Everything we have been working on together has come to fruition.

If I can offer some final advice, don't hide this book away in a cupboard and forget about it – come back to it now and again to see how well you are progressing against your goals.

And don't forget what we have been saying all along about transferable skills. In your jobsearch you have been developing a wide variety of transferable skills – active listening, interpersonal communication and networking to name just three. Transfer them with you into your new job – don't leave them in the cupboard.

New kid on the block

You get only one opportunity to create a first impression. So here are a few things to think about. I hope they will help you to take the right first steps on your new journey.

- You can choose a lot of things in life but, like you can't choose your family, you can't choose your boss! Work on building a good relationship. Identify his/her working style and standards. Find out what's important to them.

- Create the right first impression. Whether through punctuality, dress or the quality of your work, you're being watched and labels are applied very quickly and last for a long time. I was nicknamed 'Smiler' (ah well, could have been worse) at the age of 11 and am still known by that name to some of my friends! And 'do unto others . . .' – it's what I call the difference between personal power and positional power. People who rely on positional power expect others to click their heels and come running, just because they're the group chief accountant or because they're a supervisor. People with personal power get things done because of their respect for others and their ability to treat them decently.

- Set the standards. If you're unhappy with the quality of people's work then address it quickly and tactfully. If you're pleased with people's work then say so. Everyone likes praise!

- Identify and make friends with Taffy and John. Taffy was the head of security and John was the maintenance man at the last company I worked at. They had a finger on the pulse of everything that was going on in the building and could sort anything from a broken-down car to a hotel booking. I swear that if I'd needed to charter a 747, one of them would have been able to arrange it, and if they couldn't they would have known a 'man who can'!

- Read your job description and understand what's expected of you. If you haven't got one, ask for one – or better still, offer to write it!

- Ask your boss for feedback – 'How am I doing'?

- If you don't have an induction programme, ask for one. If there isn't one, then design it yourself so that in the first month you'll make contact with everyone you'll interact with during the course of your work. Which do you think is better for building productive relationships, sitting in an ivory tower and exchanging e-mails with someone you have never met or telephoning, say the production manager, and asking 'I'm new to this industry, could someone show me the production line so that I can see exactly how we make our products?'

- Don't be a shirker. Accept new challenges with enthusiasm. Clockwatchers, 9–5ers and those who shy away from work have a short 'shelf life'.

- Don't keep going on about how wonderful things were at your last company. By all means bring in new ideas but don't become a CD stuck in replay mode.

- If you're going to make changes, think through how you're going to communicate the changes, how you're going to implement them and what the impact on others will be. How will you handle their reaction? Transformational changes (we were travelling north, we did a handbrake turn and now we're going south west!) tend to ruffle more feathers than incremental changes (if we turn the wheel gently then . . .). There's a place for both kinds of change, but for both think it through, then follow through.

Good luck in your new job.

I wish you every success.

'When you win . . . nothing hurts.'

Joe Nameth, New York Jets

Thank you

This book would never have become a reality without the help, support and advice of a great number of people. I am especially grateful to the thousands of career and life planners and jobsearchers who have bought the previous editions of *3 Easy Steps to the Job You Want* over the years. Knowing how useful the information and exercises have been to them was the inspiration to write my first book, and has sustained me through many long hours at my desk as I have written each new edition.

I am also grateful to the 30 critical readers whose invaluable advice helped me in the development of *Get That Job!*. Thank you also to Professor Dave Bartram of SHL plc, Bob Edenborough of ASE, Simon Parker at monster.co.uk, and Andrew Banks and Geoff Morgan, all of whom have been kind enough to contribute articles, and to Richard who did the illustrations.

Thank you to my editor, Rachael Stock, at Pearson Education for her advice and guidance.

Final thanks go to Bernie, my wife, for her help and support throughout the project, and to Sadie who reminded me of the benefits of taking a break occasionally, to 'stop and smell the roses'. (Sadie is our German Shepherd dog)

I have made every effort to make the text of this book non-discriminatory. If I have failed in any part, please accept my apologies and let me know, so that I can correct it for future editions.

Share these lessons with others

Malcolm Hornby frequently speaks, throughout the UK, on all of the aspects of jobsearching and career & life planning covered in his books. If you would like to invite him to speak at your conference, seminar or meeting please write to him c/o Professional Division, Pearson Education, Edinburgh Gate, Harlow, Essex CM20 2JE or e-mail Malcolm@Delta-Management.co.uk

VISIT THE WEBSITE OF THIS BOOK AT
www.Get-That-Job.co.uk